Anonymous

Folklore and Legends

Russian and Polish

Anonymous

Folklore and Legends
Russian and Polish

ISBN/EAN: 9783337294687

Printed in Europe, USA, Canada, Australia, Japan

Cover: Foto ©Thomas Meinert / pixelio.de

More available books at **www.hansebooks.com**

AND

LEGENDS

RUSSIAN AND POLISH

W. W. GIBBINGS

18 BURY ST., LONDON, W.C.

1890

INTRODUCTORY NOTE.

IN this volume I present selections made from the Russian chap-book literature, and from the works of various Russian and Polish collectors of Folklore —Afanasief, Erben, Wojcicki, Glinski, etc. The chap-book tales, and many of those of Glinski, are, there is little doubt, of foreign origin, but since Russia and Poland are the countries in which these tales have found their home, and since they have there been so adapted by the people as to incorporate the national customs and lore, they appear to me to belong properly to the present volume.

C. J. T.

CONTENTS

THE POOR MAN AND THE JUDGE.

ONCE upon a time there were two brothers who lived upon a piece of ground. The one was rich and the other poor. One day the poor brother went to the rich one to ask him to lend him a horse, so that he might carry wood from the forest. The rich brother lent him the horse, and then the poor one asked him to also let him have a collar for it. The rich man, however, got angry, and would not let him have one, and then it occurred to the poor man that he could fasten the sledge to the horse's tail. Away he went to the forest to get his wood, and he got such a load that the horse could scarcely draw it. When he came home with it he opened the gate, but he did not think of the board at the foot of the gate, and the horse tumbling over it tore its tail out!

The poor fellow took the horse back to his rich brother, but he, when he saw that the horse had no tail, would not receive it, and went off to the judge Schemyaka to complain to him of the poor brother. The poor man saw that things looked bad for him, and that he would be sent for by the judge. He thought over the matter for a long time, and at last set off after his brother on foot.

On their way the two brothers had to pass over a bridge, and the poor man, thinking that he should never return from the judge alive, jumped over it. It chanced that, just at that time, a man's son was driving his sick father to the baths, and was passing under the bridge. The poor man fell upon the old man and killed him, and the son went off to the judge to complain of his father's having been killed.

The rich brother, when he came to the judge, laid his complaint before him, telling him that his brother had pulled out his horse's tail. Now the poor man had taken a stone and wrapped it in a cloth, and he stood with it in his hand, behind his brother, intending to kill the judge if he did not decide in his favour. The judge thought the man had brought a hundred roubles for him in the cloth, so he ordered the rich man to give his horse to the poor man until the tail was grown again.

Then came the son to complain to the judge of the poor man having slain his father. The poor man again took the stone wrapped in the cloth and showed it to the judge, who thought the man must there have two hundred roubles to give to him for deciding the case. So he ordered the son to take his place upon the bridge and the poor man to stand below. Then the son was to throw himself off the bridge on to the poor man and crush him to death.

The poor brother went to the rich one to take the horse without a tail, as the judge had ordered, so that he might keep it till the tail grew. The rich man, however, was not willing to lose his horse, so he gave the poor man five roubles, three bushels of corn, and a milch-goat, and so they settled the matter.

Then the poor man went off to the son, and said—

"According to the judgment you must stand on the bridge while I must stand underneath it, and then you must jump off and crush me to death."

Then thought the son—

"Who knows whether if I jump off the bridge I may not, instead of crushing him to death, kill myself?"

So he thought it would be best to come to an arrangement with the poor man, and he gave him two hundred roubles, a horse, and five bushels of corn.

After this the judge, Schemyaka, sent his servant to the poor man to ask him for two hundred roubles. The poor man showed him the stone, and said—

"If the judge had not decided for me I should have killed him with it."

When the servant came back to the judge and told him that, he crossed himself—

"Thank Heaven," said he, "I decided as he wished!"

THE WIND-RIDER.

A MAGICIAN was once upon a time much put out with a young countryman, and being in a great rage he went to the man's hut and stuck a new sharp knife under the threshold. While he did so he cursed the man, saying—

"May this fellow ride for seven years on the fleet storm-wind, until he has gone all round the world."

Now when the peasant went into the meadows in order to carry the hay, there came suddenly a gust of wind. It quickly scattered the hay, and then seized the peasant. He endeavoured in vain to resist; in vain he sought to cling to the hedges and trees with his hands. Do what he would, the invisible power hurried him forwards.

He flew on the wings of the wind like a wild pigeon, and his feet no more touched the ground. At length the sun set, and the poor fellow looked with hungry eyes upon the smoke which curled up from the chimneys in his village. He could almost touch them with his feet, but he called and screamed

4

in vain, and all his wailing and complaints were useless. No one heard his lamentation, no one saw his
tears.

So he went on for three months, and what with
thirst and hunger he was dried up and almost a
skeleton. He had gone over a good deal of ground
by that time, but the wind most often carried him
over his native village.

He wept when he saw the hut in which dwelt his
sweetheart. He could see her busied about the house.
Sometimes she would bring out some dinner in a
basket. Then he would stretch out his dried-up
hands to her, and vainly call her name. His voice
would die away, and the girl not hearing him would
not look up.

He fled on. The magician came to the door
of his hut, and seeing the man, cried to him,
mockingly—

"You have to ride for seven years yet, flying over
this village. You shall go on suffering, and shall
not die."

"O my father," said the man, "if I ever offended
you, forgive me! Look! my lips are quite hard; my
face, my hands, look at them! I am nothing but
bone. Have pity upon me."

The magician muttered a few words, and the man
stopped in his course. He stayed in one place, but
did not yet stand on the ground.

"Well, you ask me to pity you," said the magician.

"And what do you mean to give me if I put a stop to your torment?"

"All you wish," said the peasant, and he clasped his hands, and knelt down in the air.

"Will you give me your sweetheart," asked the magician, "so that I may have her for my wife? If you will give her up, you shall come to earth again."

The man thought for a moment, and said to himself—

"If I once get on the earth again, I may see if I cannot do something."

So he said to the magician—

"Indeed, you ask me to make a great sacrifice, but if it must be so it must."

The magician then blew at him, and the man came to the ground. He was very pleased to find the earth once more under his feet, and to have escaped from the power of the wind. Off he hurried to his hut, and at the threshold he met his sweetheart. She cried aloud with amazement when she saw the long-lost peasant, whom she had so long lamented and wept for. With his skinny hands the man put her gently aside, and went into the house, where he found the farmer who had employed him sitting down, and said to him, as he commenced to weep—

"I can no longer stay in your service, and I cannot marry your daughter. I love her very

much, as much as the apple of my eye, but I
cannot marry her."

The old farmer wondered to see him, and when
he saw his white pinched face and the traces of his
suffering, he asked him why he did not wish for
the hand of his daughter.

The man told him all about his ride in the air,
and the bargain he had made with the magician.
When the farmer had listened to it all, he told the
poor fellow to keep a good heart, and putting some
money in his pocket, went out to consult a sorceress.

Towards evening he returned very merry, and
taking the peasant aside, said to him—

"To-morrow morning, before day, go to the witch,
and you will find all will be well."

The wearied peasant, who had not slept for three
months, went to bed, but he woke before it was
day, and went off to the witch. He found her
sitting beside the hearth boiling herbs over a fire.
She told him to stand by her, and, suddenly,
although it was a calm day, such a storm of wind
arose that the hut shook again.

The sorceress then took the peasant outside into
the yard and told him to look up. He lifted up
his eyes, and—O wonder!—saw the evil magician
whirling round and round in the air.

"There is your enemy," said the woman, "he
will trouble you no more. If you would like to

see him at your wedding, I will tell you what to do, but he must suffer the torment that he meant to put you to."

The peasant was delighted, and ran back to the house, and a month later he was married. While the wedding folk were dancing, the peasant went out into the yard, looked up, and saw right over the hut the magician turning round and round. Then the peasant took a new knife, and throwing it with all his force, stuck it in the magician's foot.

He fell at once to the ground, and the knife held him to the earth, so that he could only stand at the window and see how merry the peasant and his friends were.

The next day he had disappeared, but he was afterwards seen flying in the air over a lake. Before him and behind him were flocks of ravens and crows, and these, with their hoarse cries, heralded the wicked magician's endless ride on the wind.

THE THREE GIFTS.

A VERY rich widow had three children, a step-son, a fine young fellow, a step-daughter of wonderful beauty, and a daughter who was not so bad. The three children lived under the same roof, and took their meals together. At length the time came when the children were treated very differently. Although the widow's daughter was bad-tempered, obstinate, vain, and a chatterer, her mother loved her passionately, praised her, and covered her with caresses. She was favoured in every way. The step-son, who was a good-natured lad, and who did all kinds of work, was for ever grumbled at, checked, and treated like a sluggard. As for the step-daughter, who was so wonderfully pretty, and who had the disposition of an angel, she was tormented, worried, and ill-treated in a thousand ways. Between her sister and her step-mother her life was made miserable.

It is natural that one should love one's own children better than those of other folk; but it is only right that liking and disliking should be

9

indulged in with moderation. The evil step-mother, however, loved her child to distraction, and equally detested her step-children. To such a pitch did she carry these feelings that when she was angry she used to say how she would advance the fortune of her daughter even at the orphans' expense.

An old proverb says, "Man sets the ball rolling, but Heaven directs it," and we shall see what happened.

One Sunday morning the step-daughter, before going to church, went out into the garden to pluck some flowers to place on the altar. She had gathered some roses, when, on lifting up her eyes, she saw, right in front of her, three young men who sat upon a grassy bank. They were clothed in garments of dazzling white which shone like sunshine. Near by them was an old man, who came and asked the girl for alms.

The girl was a little frightened when she saw the three men, but when the old man came to her she took her last piece of money out of her pocket and gave it to him. The poor man thanked her, put the piece of money into his bag, and, laying his hand on the girl's head, said to the young men—

"You see this little orphan; she is good and patient in suffering, and has so much pity for the poor that she gives them even the last penny she has. What do you wish for her?"

The first one said—

"I wish that when she cries her tears may turn to pearls."

"I wish," said the second, "that when she laughs the most delicately perfumed roses may fall from her lips."

"And I," said the third, "wish that when she touches water golden fish spring up in it."

"So shall it be," said the old man, and he and his companions vanished.

When the girl saw that, she gave thanks to Heaven, and ran joyfully into the house. Hardly had she entered when her step-mother met her and gave her a slap on the face, saying—

"Where are you running to?"

The poor girl began to cry, but behold! instead of tears pearls fell from her eyes. The step-mother forgot her rage, and set herself to gather them up as quickly as possible. The girl could not help laughing at the sight, and from her lips there fell roses of such a delightful scent that the step-mother was beside herself with pleasure. After that the girl, wishing to preserve the flowers she had plucked in the garden, poured some water into a glass : as soon as she touched the water with her finger, it was filled with beautiful golden fish.

From that time the same things never failed to happen. The girl's tears turned to pearls, when she laughed roses, which did not die, fell from her lips;

and water which she only touched with her little finger became filled with golden fish.

The step-mother became better disposed towards her, and by little and little learned from her the secret of how she had obtained these gifts.

On the following Sunday she sent her own daughter into the garden to pluck flowers as if for the altar. Hardly had the girl gathered some roses, when, lifting up her eyes, she saw the three young men sitting on a grassy bank, beautiful, and shining like the sun, and by them was the old man, clad in white, who asked her for alms. When she saw the young men, the girl pretended to be afraid, but when the old man spoke to her, she ran to him, took out of her pocket a gold piece, looked hard at it, and then gave it to him, but evidently very much against her will. The old man put the money in his bag, and said to the three others—

"You see this girl who is her mother's spoilt child? She is bad-tempered, wicked, and is hard-hearted as regards the poor. We know very well why she has been so charitable, for the first time in her life, to-day. Tell me then what you wish for her."

The first said—

" I wish that when she cries her tears may change to lizards."

" I," said the second, " wish that when she laughs, hideous toads may fall from her lips."

"And I," said the third, "wish that when she touches water with her hand it may be filled with serpents."

"It shall be as you wish," said the old man, and he and his companions disappeared.

The girl was terrified, and ran into the house to tell her mother what had happened. All occurred as had been said. When she laughed toads sprang from her lips, when she cried her tears changed to lizards, and when she touched water it became full of serpents.

The step-mother did not know what to do. She paid greater attention than ever to her daughter, and hated the orphans more and more, and so tormented them that the lad, not being able to put up with it, took leave of his sister, praying Heaven to guard her, and, leaving his step-mother's house, set out to seek his fortune. The wide world was before him. He knew not where to go, but he knew that Heaven, that sees all men, watches over the orphans. He prayed, and then walking down to the burial-ground where slept his father and mother, he knelt at the grave. He wept and prayed for a time, and having kissed the earth which covered them three times, he rose and prepared to set out on his journey. All of a sudden he · felt, in the folds of his dress on his bosom, something he had not perceived there before. He put his hand up, and was so astonished that he could scarcely believe his eyes, for he found there a charming little picture of his much-loved sister, surrounded by pearls, roses, and little golden fish. Delighted at the sight, he kissed the picture, looked around the burial-ground once more, made the sign of the cross, and set out on his way.

A story is soon told, but events move slowly.

After many adventures of little importance he came to the capital of a kingdom situated on the sea-shore. There he sought to obtain a living, and he was not unsuccessful, for he was engaged to look after the king's garden, and was both well fed and well paid. This good fortune did not, however, make him forget his poor sister, about whom he was much troubled. When he had a moment to himself, he would sit down in some quiet spot and look at his picture, sometimes melting into tears, for he looked upon the portrait of his sister as a precious legacy given to him by his parents at their grave.

One day while the lad sat thus by a brook, the king saw him, and creeping up to him from behind very softly, he looked over his shoulder at the likeness that the young man was regarding so attentively.

"Give me the portrait," said the king.

The lad gave it to him.

The king looked at it and was delighted.

"Never," said he, "in all my life did I see such a

beautiful girl, never have I heard of such a one, never did I dream there was such. Tell me, does she live?"

The lad burst into tears, and told the king that the picture was the portrait of his sister, who some time ago had been so favoured by Heaven that when she cried her tears became pearls, when she laughed roses sprang from her lips, and when she touched water it was filled with golden fish.

The king ordered him to write at once to his step-mother, to tell her to send her lovely step-daughter to his palace, where the king waited to make her his wife. On the occasion of his marriage he declared he would heap rewards on the step-mother and on the brother of his bride. The lad wrote the letter, and the king sent a servant with it.

A story is quickly told, but events move slowly.

After she had read the letter, the step-mother did not show it to the orphan, but to her own daughter.

So they plotted together, and the step-mother went to an old sorceress to consult her, and to be instructed in magic. She then set out with her two daughters. As they came near to the capital of the king's dominions, in a place near to the sea, the step-mother suddenly threw the step-daughter out of the carriage, muttered some magic words, and spat three times behind her. All at once the poor girl became very little, covered with feathers, and changed into a wild duck. She commenced to

cackle, threw herself into the sea, just as ducks do,
and began to swim about there. The step-mother
dismissed her with these words: "By the force of
my hate, I have done what I wished! Swim away
upon the shore like a duck, happy in liberty, and in
the meantime my daughter, clothed in your beauty,
shall marry the king, and enjoy all that was meant
for you."

Hardly had she finished these words when her
daughter found herself clothed in all the charms of
the unfortunate girl. So they went on their way,
came to the palace, which they reached at the time
named in the letter, and there the king received the
daughter from the hands of the treacherous step-
mother, in place of the orphan. After the marriage,
the step-mother, loaded with presents, returned to
her home. The king, looking upon his wife, could
not imagine how it was that he did not feel that
love and tenderness that had been aroused in him at
the sight of the portrait. However, there was no
remedy, what was done was done. Heaven sees
one, and knows of what malady one shall die, and
what woman one shall marry! The king admired
his wife's beauty, and thought of the pleasure he
would have when he saw the pearls drop from her
eyes, the roses from her lips, and the golden fish
spring up in the water she touched. During the
feast, however, the queen chanced to laugh at her
husband, and a mass of hideous toads sprang forth!

The king ran off quickly. Then the queen commenced to cry, and instead of pearls, lizards dropped from her eyes. An attendant presented a basin of water to her, but she had no sooner dipped the tip of her finger in the water than it became a mass of serpents, which began to hiss and dart into the middle of the wedding party. Every one was afraid, and all was in confusion. The guards were at last called in, and by their aid the hall was cleared of the horrible reptiles.

The king had gone into the garden, where he met with the orphan lad ; and so enraged was the king at the trick that he thought had been played him, that he gave the lad a blow on the head with his stick. The poor lad, falling down upon the ground, died at once.

The queen came running to the king, sobbing, and, taking him by the hand, said—

"What have you done? You have killed my brother, who was altogether guiltless. Is it his fault or mine that, since I have been married to you, I have lost the wonderful powers I once had? They will come back again in time, but time will not bring my brother to me more."

"Pardon me, my dear wife," said the king. "In a moment of rage I thought he had betrayed me, and I wished to punish him. I am sorry for what I have done ; now, however, it is beyond recall. Forgive me, and I forgive you with all my heart."

"I pardon you," said the queen, "but I beg you to order that my brother shall be honourably buried."

The queen's wish was carried out. The poor lad, who was thought to be the queen's brother, was put in a fine coffin, and laid on a magnificent catafalque in the church. When night came on a guard of honour was placed around the coffin and at the gates to watch till morning. Towards midnight the doors of the church opened of their own accord and without any noise, and, at the same moment, an irresistible drowsiness came over the soldiers, who all went to sleep. A pretty little wild duck entered, stopped in the middle of the church, shook its feathers, of which it freed itself one by one, and there stood the orphan girl in her former shape. She approached the coffin of her brother, and shed very many tears over him, which all changed to pearls. After she had wept for some time, she reassumed the feathers once more, and went out. When the guards awoke, great was their surprise to find a number of beautiful pearls on the coffin. The next day they told the king how the gates of the church had opened of themselves at midnight, how an irresistible desire to sleep had overtaken them, and how the pearls had been discovered upon the coffin. The king was surprised at their story, and more so when he saw the pearls. He doubled the guard, and told them to watch more carefully the second night.

At the same time the doors opened again of
themselves, and the soldiers again fell asleep. The
wild duck entered, shook off its feathers, and
became the lovely girl. At the sight of the double
guard, all of them fast asleep, she could not help
laughing, and beautiful roses fell from her lips. As
she approached her brother her tears broke forth
and fell in a shower of pearls to the ground. At
length she took her feathers again and flew away.
When the guards awoke they collected the roses
and pearls and took them to the king, who was now
more surprised than before, seeing not only the
pearls but the roses also. He again doubled the
guards, and he threatened them with the most
severe punishment if they did not keep awake.
They did their best, but all was of no use. At the
end of their nap on the third night they found not
only pearls and roses, but also golden fish swimming in the church font. The king was now very
much astonished, and began to think that there
must be some magic in the matter. When night
came on he again doubled the number of the
guards, and hid himself in the chapel, after having
put up a mirror in which he could see everything
reflected without being himself seen.

At midnight the doors opened of themselves,
the soldiers dropt their arms, lay down on the
ground, and fell fast asleep. The king did not
take his eyes off the mirror, and he saw a little

wild duck enter, and look timidly around it. When
it saw the guards all asleep it seemed to take
courage, and came into the middle of the church.
Then it cast off its feathers and became a girl of
extraordinary loveliness. The king was transported with joy and wonder, and felt that this must
be his true bride. When she had come to the
coffin the king rushed forward with a wax taper in
his hand and set fire to the feathers, the flame
leaping up and waking the guards. When the girl
saw what was done she ran to the king wringing
her hands, while pearls dropped from her eyes.

"What have you done?" she cried. "How shall
I now escape the fury of my step-mother, by whose
magic arts I was turned into a wild duck?"

Then she told the king all, and he at once
ordered some of his guards to seize the woman who
had so treacherously married him, and to conduct
her out of the kingdom. He also sent some soldiers
to take the step-mother and burn her as a sorceress.
While the king gave these orders the girl took from
her bosom three little vessels, which she had
brought with her from the sea, full of different
liquids. She sprinkled the liquid in one of them
over her brother, and he became supple and warm;
his cheeks took their colour again, and the warm
red blood began to run from his wound. His sister
sprinkled him again with the second liquid, which
had the property of healing, and his wound at once

closed. She sprinkled him the third time with the water which had the property of calling back to life. The young man opened his eyes, looked on his sister with astonishment, and threw himself, full of happiness, into her arms.

At the sight of this the king was overjoyed. He took the young man by the hand, and, leading his sister, the three went to the palace.

In a short time he married his true bride, and he lived happily with her and her brother for many years.

SNYEGURKA.

THERE was once upon a time a peasant named Ivan, who had a wife named Mary. They had been married many years, and loved one another, but they had no children, and this caused them so much sorrow that they could find no pleasure but in watching the children of their neighbours. What could they do? Heaven had willed it so. Things in this world do not go as we wish, but as Heaven ordains.

One day, in the winter, the children played about in the road and the two old folk looked on, sitting in the window seat. At last the children began to make a beautiful snow figure. Ivan and Mary looked on enjoying it.

All of a sudden Ivan said—

"Wife, suppose we make a snow figure?"

Mary was ready.

"Why not?" said she; "we might as well amuse ourselves a little. But what is the use of making a big figure? Better make a snow-child, since God has not given us a living one."

22

"You are right," said Ivan, and he took his hat and went out into the garden with his wife.

So they set to work to make a snow-child. They fashioned a little body, little hands, and little feet, and when all that was done they rolled a snow-ball and shaped it into a head.

"Heaven bless you!" cried a passer-by.

"Thanks," replied Ivan.

"The help of Heaven is always good," said Mary.

"What are you doing?" asked the stranger.

"Look," said Ivan.

"We are making a snow-girl," said Mary.

On the ball of snow which stood for a head they made the nose and the chin. Then they put two little holes for the eyes. As Ivan finished the work, oh, wonderful! the figure became alive! He felt a warm breath come from its lips. Ivan drew back, and looked. The child had sparkling eyes, and there was a smile upon its lips.

"Heavens! what is this?" cried Ivan, making the sign of the cross.

The snow figure bent its head as if it was alive, and stirred its little arms and legs in the snow as if it was a real child.

"Ivan! Ivan!" cried Mary, trembling with joy, "Heaven has heard our prayers," and she threw herself on the child and covered her with kisses. The snow fell away from the little girl like the shell from a chicken. .

"Ah, my dear Snyegurka!" cried Mary, embracing the long wished for and unexpected child, and she carried her off into the cottage.

Ivan had much to do to recover himself, he was so surprised, and Mary was foolish with joy.

Snyegurka grew hour by hour, and became more and more beautiful. Ivan and Mary were overjoyed, and their hut was full of life and merriment. The village girls were always there playing with Snyegurka, dressing her, chattering with her, singing songs to her, teaching her all they knew. Snyegurka was very clever; she noticed everything, and learnt things quickly. During that winter she grew as big as a three-year-old child. She understood things, and when she spoke her voice was so sweet that one could have listened to it for ever. She was amiable, obedient, and affectionate. Her skin was white, her hair the colour of flax, and her eyes deep blue; her cheeks, however, had no rosy flush in them, for she had no blood, but she was so good and so amiable that every one loved her.

"You see," said Mary, "what joy has Heaven given us in our old age."

"Heaven be thanked," responded Ivan.

At last the winter was ended, and the spring sun shone down and warmed the earth. The snow melted, the green grass sprang up in the fields, and the lark sang high up in the sky. The village girls went singing—

"Sweet spring, how did you come to us?
How did you come?
Did you come on a plough, or on a harrow?"

Snyegurka, however, became very sad. "What is the matter with you, my dear child?" said Mary, drawing her to her and caressing her. "Are you not well? You are not merry. Has an evil eye glanced on you?"

"No," answered Snyegurka; "it is nothing, mother. I am quite well."

The last snow of the winter had melted and disappeared. Flowers sprang up in all the gardens and fields. In the woods the nightingale and all the birds sang, and all the world seemed very happy save Snyegurka, who became more and more sad. She would run away from her companions, and hide herself from the sun in dark nooks, like a timid flower under the trees. She liked nothing save playing by the water-side under the green willows. She seemed to enjoy only the cool and the shower. At nighttime she was happy; and when a good storm occurred, a fierce hail-storm, she was as pleased with the drops as if they had been pearls. When the sun broke forth again—when the hail was melted—then Snyegurka began to weep bitterly.

The spring was ended, the summer came, and the feast of Saint John was at hand. The girls were going to play in the woods, and they called for Snyegurka to go with them.

Mary was afraid to let her go, but she thought
that the outing might do her child good, so she got
her ready, embraced her, and said—

"Go, my child, and play with your friends; and
you, my daughters, look well after her. You know
I love her better than the apple of my eye."

"All right," cried they all, and they ran off in a
body to the woods.

There they plucked the wild-flowers, made themselves wreaths, and sang songs.

When the sun was setting they made a fire of
dry grass and placed themselves in a row by it,
each of them having a crown of flowers on her head.
"Look at us," said they to Snyegurka, "how we
run, and follow us," and then they began to sing
and to jump, around and over the little fire.

All of a sudden they heard, behind them, a sigh—
"Ah!"

They looked about them, and then at one another.
There was nothing to be seen. They looked again,
and found that Snyegurka was no longer among
them.

"She has hidden herself," cried they. Then they
looked for her, but could not find her, calling out
and shouting her name, but there was no answer.

"Where can she be? She must have gone home,"
said they.

They ran back to the village, but there no one
had seen Snyegurka. All the folk searched during

the next day and the day following. They went through all the woods, they looked through every thicket, but no trace of the child was discovered.

Ivan and Mary were inconsolable, and for a long time did the poor mother seek her child in the woods, crying—

" Snyegurka, my sweet, come to me."

Sometimes she thought she could hear the voice of her child replying to her; but no, it was not Snyegurka.

" What could have become of her?" folk asked one another; " can a wild beast have carried her off into the woods? Has some bird of prey flown off with her? "

No beast had carried her off, nor had a bird flown away with her. When she began to run with her companions she suddenly changed into a light vapour, and was carried up to heaven.

PRINCE PETER AND PRINCESS MAGILENE.

IN the kingdom of France there was once a high-born prince named Volchvan who married a noble lady named Petronida. They had one son, who was called Peter. This Prince Peter in his youth was very fond of horsemanship and of war, and when he grew up he thought of nothing but knightly deeds. Now it chanced that just at that time there arrived a knight named Ruiganduis, who had come from Naples, and he, seeing the Prince's disposition, said to him, "Prince Peter, the King of Naples has a beautiful daughter named Magilene, and he bestows great rewards on the knights who by their deeds do honour to her."

Peter, when he heard that, went to his father and mother, and begged them to let him go to Naples to learn knightly arts, and, especially, to see the beautiful Magilene, the daughter of the King.

They parted with Prince Peter with great sorrow, and bade him only make friends of good folk. Then they gave him three gold rings with precious stones, and also a golden key. So they sent him off.

23

When Prince Peter came to Naples he went to a clever workman, and ordered him to make him a coat of mail, and a helmet to match, and told him to fasten to it two golden keys. When he had done this he rode away to the place where the tournaments were held, where he found the King. The folk called Peter, Peter with the Golden Keys, and off he went and placed himself among the knights. First of all there rode out the Knight Andrei Skrintor, and against him appeared the son of the King of England. Andrei dealt Henry such a blow, that he was nearly thrown off his horse. Then Landiot, the King's son, came forth and threw Andrei off his horse on to the ground.

When Prince Peter saw that Landiot had thrown Andrei from his saddle, he rode out and cried aloud—

"Long may their Majesties live in happiness, the King, the Queen, and their beautiful daughter, the Princess Magilene."

He rode at Landiot with such force that his horse rolled on the ground and the spear went through his heart. This deed won for him the praise of the King and of all the knights, but especially that of the Princess Magilene, and Prince Peter became the first of all the King's knights.

Now when the beautiful Princess saw how brave and handsome Prince Peter was she fell in love with him, and resolved to marry him. She made a

confidante of her maid, and from that time Prince
Peter used to see the Princess daily. He gave her
the three golden rings as a mark of his true love,
and one day, taking her with him, rode away from
the city.

They rode off on their good horse, taking much
gold and silver with them, and they continued their
journey all night. At length they came to a thick
forest which stretched far away to the seashore.
There they stopped to rest, and the Princess, lying
down on the grass, fell fast asleep. Prince Peter
sat by her side and watched her, and as he looked
at her he saw a locket having a golden fastening.
He opened it and out fell the three gold rings he
had given to her. The Prince put them on the grass,
and, as it chanced, a black raven flew by at the
moment, seized the rings, and took them off into a
tree. Peter climbed up the tree, hoping to catch
the bird; but as he was about to seize it, the raven
flew into another tree, and so from tree to tree till
at last it went away over the sea to an island, letting
the rings fall into the water.

Prince Peter followed the bird, and, having come
to the seashore, he looked about him for a boat in
which he could pursue it to the island. At length
he set off in a small fishing-boat, but as he had no
oars he paddled along with his hands. All of a
sudden, as he was on his way, there came on a
storm of wind which carried him away to the open

sea. When the Prince saw he was far from the shore he thought he was lost, and he prayed with groans and tears.

"Alas! I am the most miserable and unfortunate of all men," said he. "Why did I not leave the rings in the locket where they were safe? No one in the world is so unfortunate as I, for I have lost my happiness. I have led the Princess away, and have left her in the thick forest, where wild beasts will tear her in pieces, or she will wander about till she dies of hunger. I am her destroyer, and have spilt innocent blood!" He then began to sink in the sea.

As it chanced, a vessel came by, bound from Turkey, and when the sailors saw a man floating on the sea, they took him on board, and, carrying him away to Alexandria, they sold him to a Turkish Pasha, who sent him off as a present to the Sultan. When the Sultan saw how good his behaviour was, and how agreeable he was, he made him one of his counsellors, and his honesty and his good nature won him the love of all who came in contact with him.

When the Princess awoke she found herself in the thick forest. She looked on every side, and when she could not see Prince Peter, she was much distressed, and sank down upon the ground. Then she went into the wood, and called with all her strength—

"My dear husband, Prince Peter, where are you ? "

She wandered on a long way until she met a nun, with whom she exchanged clothes, putting on the nun's dark garments and giving her her own light-coloured dress. Then she went on to a port, where she went on board a vessel which was about to sail to the country over which Prince Peter's father ruled. When she came there she went to live with a noble lady named Susanna, and, finding a place among the mountains, she made a harbour, built a convent there named after the apostles Peter and Paul, and there she also founded a hospital for strangers. So she became famous for her pious works. One day the father and mother of Prince Peter came to her and brought to her three rings. They told her that their cook had purchased a fish in which the rings had been found. These rings they had given to their son Peter, and they therefore concluded that he had been drowned, and they wept bitterly.

Now when Peter had been with the Sultan a long time, he wished to visit his own land, and the Sultan gave him his leave to go, loading him, at the same time, with presents of gold, silver, and magnificent pearls. Having taken leave of the Sultan, the Prince went and hired a French vessel, bought fourteen casks, put salt at the bottom of them, laid the gold and silver in the casks, scattered more salt on the top of the treasure, and told the sailors that there was nothing but salt in the casks. The wind was favourable, and they set off for the Prince's land, and, having arrived at an island not far off the coast of France, they weighed anchor, for the Prince was very sea-sick. He went upon shore and wandered about in the island till he lost his way, and being tired he lay down and went to sleep. He slept a long time, and the sailors sought him and called him everywhere, but as they could not find him they set sail. They came to the Princess's convent, and there they sold the salt. Now one day when salt was wanted Magilene went to the casks and was very much surprised to find in them all the treasure.

Prince Peter was picked up by another vessel and came likewise to the convent. There he was in Magilene's hospital for a month, but all that time he did not recognise the Princess, for her black veil hid her features from him. While he was there he wept every day.

One day as Magilene came into the hospital she saw the Prince weeping, and she asked him why he did so, and he told her all his misfortunes. Magilene then recognised him, and sent off to his father and mother to tell them that their son was come back. When they came to the convent they found the Princess arrayed in her royal garments; and when the Prince saw his parents he fell at their feet, embraced them and wept, while they wept with him. At length he stood up, and, taking them by the hand, kissed them, and said—

"My father and my mother, this lady is the daughter of the great King of Naples on account of whom I left you."

So they were married, and they lived in great happiness.

THE OLD MAN, HIS WIFE, AND THE FISH.

THERE once lived in a hut on the shores of the Isle of Buyan an old man and his wife. They were very poor. The old man used to go to the sea daily to fish, and they only just managed to live on what he caught. One day he let down his net and drew it in. It seemed to be very heavy. He dragged and dragged, and at last got it to shore. There he found that he had caught one little fish of a kind he had never before seen—a golden fish.

The fish spoke to him in a man's voice. "Do not keep me, old man," it said; "let me go once more free in the sea and I will reward you for it, for whatever you wish I will do."

The old man thought for a while. Then he said, "Well, I don't want you. Go into the sea again," and he threw the fish into the water and went home.

"Well," said his wife, when he got home, "what have you caught to-day?"

35

"Only one little fish," said the man, "a golden
fish, and that I let go again, it begged so hard.
' Put me in the blue sea again,' it said, ' and I will
reward you, for whatever you wish I will do.' So
I let it go, and did not ask anything."

"Ah, you old fool ! " said the wife in a great rage,
" what an opportunity you have lost. You might,
at least, have asked the fish to give us some bread.
We have scarce a crust in the house."

The old woman grumbled so much that her
husband could have no quiet, so to please her off
he went to the seashore, and there he cried out—

> "Little fish, little fish, come now to me,
> Your tail in the water, your head out of sea ! "

The fish came to the shore.

" Well, what do you want, old man ? " it asked.

" My wife," said the man, " is in a great passion,
and has sent me to ask for bread."

" Very well," said the fish, " go home and you
shall have it."

The old man went back, and when he entered the
hut he found bread in plenty.

" Well," said he to his wife, " we have enough
bread now."

" Oh yes ! " said she, " but I have had such a misfortune while you were away. I have broken the
bucket. What shall I do the washing in now ? Go
to the fish, and ask it to give us a new bucket."

Away went the man.   Standing on the shore he called out—

> "Little fish, little fish, come now to me,
> Your tail in the water, your head out of sea!"

The fish soon made its appearance.

"Well, old man," it said, "what do you want?"

"My wife," said the man, "has had a misfortune, and has broken our bucket.   So I have come to ask for a new one."

"Very well," said the fish, "you shall find one at home."

The old man went back.   As soon as he got home his wife said to him—

"Be off to the golden fish again, and ask it to give us a new hut.   Ours is all coming to pieces. We have scarcely a roof over our heads."

The old man once more came to the shore, and cried—

> "Little fish, little fish, come now to me,
> Your tail in the water, your head out of sea!"

The fish came.

"Well, what is it?" asked the fish.

"My wife," said the man, "is in a very bad temper, and has sent me to ask you to build us a new cottage.   She says she cannot live any longer in our present one."

"Oh, do not be troubled about that," said the fish. "Go home.   You shall have what you want."

The old man went back again, and in the place of
his miserable hovel he found a new hut built of oak
and nicely ornamented. The old man was delighted,
but as soon as he went in his wife set on him, saying—

"What an idiot you are!   You do not know how
to take good fortune when it is offered to you.   You
think you have done a great thing just because you
have got a new hut.   Be off again to the golden fish,
and tell it I will not be a mere peasant's wife any
longer.   I will be an Archduchess, with plenty of
servants, and set the fashion."

The old man went to the golden fish.

"What is it?" asked the fish.

"My wife will not let me rest," replied the man;
"she wants now to be an Archduchess, and is not
content with being my wife."

"Well, it shall be as she wishes.   Go home again,"
said the fish.

Away went the man.   How astonished was he,
when, on coming to where his house had stood, he now
found a fine mansion, three stories high.   Servants
crowded the hall, and cooks were busy in the
kitchens.   On a seat in a fine room sat the man's
wife, dressed in robes shining with gold and silver,
and giving orders.

"Good day, wife!" said the man.

"Who are you, man?" said his wife.   "What
have you to do with me, a fine lady?   Take the

clown away," said she to her servants. "Take him
to the stable, and whip some of the impudence out
of him."

The servants seized the old man, took him off to
the stable, and when they had him there beat him
so that he hardly knew whether he was alive or not.
After that the wife made him the door-keeper of the
house. She gave him a besom, and put him to keep
the yard in order. ⸱ As for his meals, he got them in
the kitchen. He had a hard life of it. If the yard
was not swept clean, he had to look out.

"Who would have thought she had been such a
hag?" said the old man to himself. "Here she has
all such good fortune, and will not even own me for
her husband!"

After a time the wife got tired of being merely
an Archduchess, so she said to her husband—

"Go off to the golden fish, and tell it I will be a
Czarina."

The old man went down to the shore. He
cried—

> "Little fish, little fish, come now to me,
> Your tail in the water, your head out of sea!"

The fish came swimming to the shore.

"Well, old man!" it said, "what do you
want?"

"My wife is not yet satisfied," said the man;
"she wants now to be a Czarina."

"Do not let that trouble you," said the fish,
"but go to your house. What you ask shall be
done."

The man went back. In place of the fine house
he found a palace with a roof of gold. Soldiers were
on guard around it. In front of the palace was a
garden, and at the back a fine park, in which some
troops were parading. On a balcony stood the
Czarina surrounded by officers and nobles. The
troops presented arms, the drums beat, the trumpets
blew, and the people shouted.

In a short time the woman got tired of being
Czarina, and she commanded that her husband
should be found and brought to her presence. The
palace was all in confusion, for who knew what had
become of the old man? Officers and noblemen
hurried here and there to search for him. At length
he was found in a hut behind the palace.

"Listen, you old idiot!" said his wife. "Go to
the golden fish, and tell it that I am tired of being
Czarina. I want to rule over all the ocean, to have
dominion over every sea and all the fish."

The old man hesitated to go to the fish with such
a request.

"Be off!" said his wife, "or your head shall be
cut off."

The man went to the seashore and said—

"Little fish, little fish, come now to me,
Your tail in the water, your head out of sea!"

The fish did not come. The man waited, but it was not to be seen. Then he said the words a second time. The waves roared. A short while before it had been bright and calm, now dark clouds covered the sky, the wind howled, and the water seemed of an inky blackness.

At length the fish came.

"What do you want, old man?" it asked.

"My old wife," answered he, "is not satisfied even now. She says she will be Czarina no longer, but will rule over all the waters and all the fish."

The fish made no reply, but dived down and disappeared in the sea.

The man went back. What had become of the palace? He looked around, but could not see it. He rubbed his eyes in wonder. On the spot where the palace had stood was the old hut, and at the door stood the old woman in her old rags.

So they commenced to live again in their old style. The man often went a-fishing, but he never more caught the golden fish.

THE GOLDEN MOUNTAIN.

IN a certain kingdom there once lived a Czar and his wife who had three fine sons. The eldest was called Vasili, the second Fedor, and the youngest Ivan. One day the Czar went with his wife to walk in his garden, and there suddenly came on such a storm that the Czarina was carried off by it, out of her husband's sight. The Czar was sore grieved, and sorrowed for a long time. When the two eldest sons saw their father's trouble they came to him, and asked him to let them go forth to look for their mother. So he gave them his blessing, and they set out. They travelled for a long time, and at last came to a great desert. There they pitched their tent, and waited to see if any one would come to tell them the way. For three years they waited, but they saw no one.

Meanwhile the youngest brother, Ivan, went to his father to ask him for his blessing, and took leave of him. He travelled for a long time, until at last he saw some tents in the distance. He rode on, and on coming to them he saw that he had found his brothers.

"Why do you stop on the borders of this dreary waste, brothers?" said he; "let us go on together and seek our mother."

The others agreed, and they once more set out. When they had gone a long way they saw in the distance a palace built of crystal, with a wall around it of the same material. They drew near to it, and Ivan opened the gate and rode into the courtyard. As he approached the door he saw a pillar to which there were attached two rings, one of gold and the other of silver. He put his bridle through the rings and secured his horse, and then went to the door. There the king of the palace came to meet him. They talked for some time, and the king, discovering that Ivan was his nephew, led him into his room, and brought his brothers in also.

When they had been with him a long time, the king gave them a magic ball, which the brothers threw before them, and following it they came to a high mountain at the foot of which they stopped to rest. It was so high and so steep that no one could climb up it. Ivan rode round it to discover some means of getting to the top, and at last he found a crevice into which he stepped. Then he saw an iron door with an iron ring. When he had opened the door he found some iron hooks which he fastened to his hands and feet. By means of these he contrived to climb to the top of the mountain. When he reached the top he was very tired, and sat down

to rest, and as soon as ever he took off the hooks
they vanished. Afar off in the mountain he saw a
tent of fine cambric, on which was pictured a copper
kingdom, and on its summit was a copper ball. On
going to the tent he found at the entrance two large
lions, which refused to let him pass. Ivan, however,
saw two copper basins standing near, so he went
and got some water and gave it to the lions, who
were thirsty, and then they let him go into the
tent. When he had come there he saw a lovely
princess on a couch, and at her feet slept a
dreadful dragon, whose head Ivan cut off with
one blow. The princess thanked him, and gave
him a copper egg, in which was contained a
copper kingdom. Then the Czarewitch left her and
went on.

When he had gone a long way he saw a
tent of fine gauze hung from a cedar-tree by silver
cords. These cords had tassels of emeralds, and on
the tent was the picture of a silver kingdom. On
the summit of the tent was a silver ball. At the
entrance lay two large tigers. He satisfied·their
thirst, as he had done that of the lions, and then
they let him pass. When he came into the tent
he saw a lovely princess dressed in very fine clothes,
and very much more beautiful than the former. At
her feet lay a dragon with six heads, and twice as
large as the first. With one blow Ivan cut off its
heads, and the princess rewarded his courage by

giving him a silver egg, in which was a silver kingdom. Then Ivan left her and went on.

At length he came to a third tent of silk, on which was pictured a golden kingdom, and on its summit was a ball of pure gold. The tent was hung from a laurel-tree by gold cords, and the tassels of the cords were composed of diamonds. By the entrance lay two large crocodiles which breathed out great flames. The Czarewitch gave them some water, and thus got them to let him enter the tent. Inside he found on a couch a princess who even surpassed the two former ones in beauty. At her feet lay a dragon with twelve heads. Ivan cut off all the heads with one blow of his sword, and the princess, thanking him, gave him a golden egg, in which was a golden kingdom. With it she also gave him her heart. As they talked together, Ivan asked the princess if she could tell him where he should find his mother, and she, showing him where his mother dwelt, wished he would have good fortune in his adventure.

He went on a long way and came to a palace, and going in he passed through many rooms, but he found no one in them. At last he came to a large beautiful hall, and there he saw his mother, dressed in royal robes, sitting on a chair. When they had tenderly saluted, Ivan told her how he and his brothers had travelled very far to seek her whom they loved so much. The Czarina informed

Ivan that a spirit would soon come, and told him to conceal himself under her cloak.

"When the spirit appears," said she, "seize his magic wand with both hands. He will then fly upwards with you, but do not be afraid, and be quiet. After a time he will fall to the earth and be dashed to pieces. You must gather these up, burn them, and scatter the ashes on the field."

His mother had scarcely finished these words, and hidden him under her cloak, before the spirit appeared. Then Ivan sprang forward as his mother had told him, and laid hold of the magic wand. The spirit seized the Czarewitch, flew with him far up, fell to the ground, and was dashed to pieces. The Czarewitch gathered these together, and burnt them, but kept the magic stick. Then he took his mother and the three princesses whom he had rescued, and, coming to an oak-tree, he let each one of them slide down the mountain-side by means of a linen cloth. When the brothers, who waited at the foot of the mountain, saw that he alone remained on the top, they tore the linen cloth out of his hand, led away their mother and the three princesses to their own kingdom, and made them take an oath that they would tell their father that they had been saved by them.

Ivan was thus left alone on the mountain, and did not know how he could get down. He walked about very sorrowfully, and happening to pass the

magic wand from one hand to the other, a man
suddenly appeared before him, and said—

"What is your will, Ivan Czarewitch?"

Ivan was much astonished to see the man, and
asked him who he was, and how he had come on
the mountain.

"I am a spirit," replied the man, "and was the
servant of him whom you have overcome. As you
have now his magic stick, and as you have passed
it from one hand to the other, as you always must
when you want me, I have come to perform what
you wish."

"That is well," said Ivan to the spirit. "Do me
your first service, then, and carry me into my own
country."

Scarcely had he finished these words before he
found himself in his father's city.

He wanted to first know what was going on in the
palace, so instead of going straight in he went and
began work in a shoemaker's shop, for he thought no
one would quickly recognise him there. The next
morning the shoemaker went into town to buy some
leather, and came home in the evening very drunk.
So tipsy was he that he could not see to the shop,
so he left all to his new man. Ivan knew nothing
about the work, so he called the spirit to assist him,
and told him to set to and make some shoes while
he himself went to sleep. When the master awoke
early the next morning he went to see what work

his man had done, and when he found him still fast
asleep, he was very angry, and said—

"Ah! you lazy fellow, do you think I took you
into my service to sleep?"

"Do not blame me," replied Ivan, stretching himself, "go first into the work-room, and see what you
find there."

The shoemaker went off, and how much was he
astonished to find there a number of shoes all
finished. He went to them and took up a shoe to
look at the work, but he was more astonished still,
and began to disbelieve his eyes, for there was not a
single stitch in the shoes, but they were all of one
piece. He took some of the shoes and set off to sell
them, and every one who saw the wonderful shoes
bought them eagerly. His fame spread, and in a
short time the shoemaker became so noted that they
sent for him to the palace. There he saw the
princesses, who ordered him to make them some
dozens of shoes, adding that they must all be ready
by the next morning. He told them that it was
impossible for him to do what they asked, but they
said that if he did not do what they told him he
should have his head cut off, for they declared they
well knew he made his shoes by some magic
means.

The poor shoemaker left the castle, thinking he
was as good as a dead man, went into the city,
bought some leather, and went a-drinking to drive

off care. Towards evening he came home, and throwing the leather down upon the floor, said to his new man—

"Listen, you wretched fellow, to what you have done with your magic work."

So he told him all that had happened with the princesses, and how he was to be put to death if he did not do what they commanded.

"Don't be put out," said Ivan; "lie down and go to sleep. The morning will bring us good luck."

His master thanked him for what he said, laid himself down on a bench, and very quickly began to snore. Then Ivan called upon his spirit, ordered him to make all ready, and went to sleep himself."

Though the shoemaker had been very drunk, when he awoke early in the morning he remembered that he was to have his head cut off that day. So he went to his man and said—

"Let us have a bottle together, so that I may be more courageous when I am under the axe."

"Do not fear," answered Ivan; "go into your workshop. You will find that all is finished, and ready to be taken to the palace."

The shoemaker walked off to the workshop, not believing what Ivan said; but when he saw all the shoes ready, he was so delighted that he did not know what to do. He embraced Ivan and called him his saviour.

He took the shoes and set off to the palace; and

when the princesses saw the shoes, they felt sure
that Ivan must be in the town, so they said to the
shoemaker—

"You have well performed what you were ordered,
but you must do something more for us. This night
there must be built opposite our palace a golden
castle. There must be a porcelain bridge from the
one palace to the other, and this must be covered
with velvet."

The shoemaker was confounded at this, and said—

"I am only a poor shoemaker, how can I do such
a thing?"

"If you do not do what we tell you," said the
princesses, "your head shall be cut off."

The shoemaker went at once from the castle,
weeping bitterly. He turned in at an alehouse to
drown his care, got drunk, and when he reached
home told Ivan what he had been commanded.

"Go to sleep," said Ivan; "to-morrow will bring
us good luck."

The shoemaker laid himself down on a bench and
went to sleep, and Ivan, calling the spirit to him,
told him to get everything ready as the shoemaker
had been commanded. After that he lay down, and
went to sleep also.

Early the next morning Ivan woke his master,
and putting the wing of a goose in his hand, said—

"Go at once to the bridge and dust it."

Ivan himself went into the golden palace. The

Czar and his daughters woke very early, and came out on the balcony, and from there they saw everything. The princesses were beside themselves with joy, for they were now sure that Ivan was in the town, and soon after they saw him standing at a window in the golden castle. Then they begged the Czar and his wife to go with them into the castle, and as they were about to go up the steps of the palace, Ivan came out to meet them. His mother and the princesses ran forward to embrace him, and said—

"This is he who rescued us."

His brothers were ashamed, and looked down on the ground, and the Czar was thunderstruck, so astonished was he. His wife, however, soon explained everything to him, and then the Czar was so angry with his eldest sons that he would have put them to death. Ivan threw himself at his feet, and said—

"My dear father, if you wish to reward me for my labour, grant me the lives of my brothers, and I shall be satisfied."

Then his father raised him up, kissed him, and said —

"They are really unworthy of thee."

So they all went back to the castle.

The following day three weddings were celebrated. The eldest son, Vasili, wedded the princess of the copper kingdom. Fedor, the second son, married the princess of the silver kingdom, and Ivan saw them settled in their dominions. He himself and his princess took possession of the golden kingdom. He took the shoemaker with him, and there they all lived for many years prosperous and happy.

THE DUCK THAT LAID GOLDEN EGGS.

THERE lived once an old man and his wife. The man was called Abrosim, and his wife Fetinia. They were very poor and miserable, and had a son named Little Ivan, who was fifteen years old. One day old Abrosim brought a crust of bread home for his wife and son. He had scarcely begun to eat, however, when Krutschina (Sorrow) sprang up from behind the stove, seized the crust out of his hand, and ran away behind the stove again. The old man made a bow to Krutschina, and begged her to give him the crust back again, as he and his wife had nothing else to eat.

"I will not give you the crust again," said Krutschina, "but instead of it I will give you a duck which lays a gold egg every day."

"Very well," said Abrosim. "I shall be supperless to-night. Do not deceive me, but tell me where I shall find the duck."

"Early to-morrow morning," said Krutschina, "when you are up, go into the town; there you will see a duck in a pond, catch it, and carry it home."

When Abrosim heard this he lay down and went to sleep.

The next morning he rose early, and went to the town, and was very much pleased to see the duck swimming about on a pond. He called it to him, carried it off to his home, and gave it to his wife Fetinia. They were both delighted, and put the duck in a big basin, placing a sieve over it. In an hour's time they went to look at it, and discovered that the duck had laid a golden egg. Then they took the duck out, and let it walk a little on the floor, and the old man, taking the egg, set off to town. There he sold the egg for a hundred roubles, took the money, and, going to the market, bought different kinds of vegetables and set off home.

The next day the duck laid another egg like the first, which Abrosim sold in the same manner. So the duck went on laying a golden egg every day, and the old man became, in a short time, very rich. He bought a large house, a great many shops, all kinds of wares, and set up in business.

His wife Fetinia made a favourite of a young clerk in her husband's employ, and used to supply him with money. One day when Abrosim was away from home, buying some goods, the clerk called to have a talk with Fetinia, and it chanced that he then saw the duck that laid the golden eggs. He was pleased with the bird, and, examining it, found written under its wing in gold letters—

" Whoever eats this duck will be a Czar."

He did not say anything to Fetinia about what
he had seen, but asked her to roast the duck for
him. Fetinia said she could not kill the duck, for
all their fortune depended on it, but the clerk
begged her so earnestly that she at last consented
and killed it, and put it in the oven. The clerk
then went off saying he would return soon, and
Fetinia also went out in the town. While they
were gone in came little Ivan. He felt very
hungry, and, looking about him for something to
eat, he chanced to see the roast duck in the oven,
so he took it out and ate all of it but the bones.
Then he went off again to the shop.

In a little while the clerk came back, and, having
called Fetinia, asked her to bring out the duck.
The woman went to the oven, but when she saw
that the duck was not there, she was terribly put
out, and told the clerk that the duck had disappeared.
At that the clerk flew into a great rage, and said—

" You have eaten the duck yourself, of course,"
and he got up and walked out of the house.

In the evening Abrosim and his son, Little Ivan,
came home. When Abrosim did not see the duck,
he asked his wife where it was, and she told him
that she did not know. Then Little Ivan said to
his father—

" My dear father, when I came home, in the
middle of the day, for dinner, my mother was not

in, so I looked in the oven, and there found a roast
duck. I took it out and ate it all but the bones,
but I do not know whether it was our duck or a
strange one."

Then old Abrosim was in such a rage that he
thrashed his wife till she was half dead, and he
turned Little Ivan out of doors.

Little Ivan began his journey. Where should
he go? He determined to follow his nose. For
ten days and nights he went on. Then he came to
a town, and as he stepped to the gate he saw a
great many people assembled together. Now these
folk had been taking council, their Czar being dead,
as to who should succeed him. In the end they
agreed that the first person who came in at the
city gate should be made Czar. Just then in came
Little Ivan through the gate, so all the people cried
out together—

" Here is our Czar ! "

The chief folk took Little Ivan by the arms,
conducted him to the royal apartments, put on him
the Czar's robes, seated him on the throne, made
obeisance to him as to their Czar, and waited for
his commands. Then Little Ivan thought he must
surely be asleep and dreaming all this ; but at last
he knew that he must be really Czar. He was
heartily pleased, began to rule over the people, and to
appoint his officers. A short time after he called
one of them, named Luga, to him, and said—

"My true friend and good knight Luga, I want you to do me a service. Go to my own country, go to the Czar, salute him from me, and ask him to deliver to you the shopkeeper Abrosim and his wife, so that you may bring them to me. If he will not deliver them up to you, tell him that I will lay waste his country with fire, and will make him himself my prisoner."

When the servant Luga was come into Little Ivan's country he went to the Czar and asked him to let Abrosim and Fetinia go away with him. The Czar was unwilling to let Abrosim go, for he wanted to keep the rich merchant in his own country. He knew, however, that Ivan's kingdom was very large and populous, and being therefore afraid, he let Abrosim and Fetinia depart. Luga received them from the Czar, and conducted them to his own native country.

When he brought them to Little Ivan, the Czar said to his father—

"Yes, father, you turned me away from your house, and I therefore bring you to mine. Come, live with me, you and my mother, till the end of your days."

Abrosim and Fetinia rejoiced exceedingly to find that their son was become Czar, and they lived with him many years, until they died.

Little Ivan ruled for thirty years in good health, and was very happy, and all his people loved him sincerely to the last hour of his life.

EMELYAN THE FOOL.

IN a certain village there once lived a peasant who had three sons, of whom two were sensible, but the third was a fool, and his name was Emelyan. When the peasant had lived for a long time, and was grown very old, he called his three sons to him, and said to them—

"My dear children, I feel that I have not very long to live, so I give you the house and cattle, which you will divide, share and share alike, among you. I also leave you, in money, a hundred roubles apiece."

Soon after the old man died, and his sons, after they had buried him, lived on happy and contented.

Some time after Emelyan's brothers took it into their heads to remove into the city, and carry on trade with the three hundred roubles which their father had left them. So they said to Emelyan—

"Hark ye, fool! we are going to the city, and we will take your hundred roubles with us, and if we prosper in trade we will buy you a red coat, red boots, and a red cap. Do you, however, stay at home here, and when your sisters-in-law desire you to do anything, do as they bid you."

The fool, who had a great longing for a red coat, a red cap, and red boots, answered at once that he would do whatever his sisters-in-law told him. So his brothers went off to the city, and Emelyan stayed at home.

One day, when the winter was come and the cold was great, his sisters-in-law told him to go out and fetch in water, but Emelyan remained lying on the stove, and said—

"Ay, and who, then, are you?"

"How now, fool!" said his sisters-in-law, "we are what you see. You know how cold it is, and that it is a man's business to go."

"I am lazy," replied he.

"How!" cried they. "You are lazy! You will want to eat, and how can we cook if we have no water? Very well, then, we will tell our husbands not to give him anything when they have bought the fine red coat and all for him."

The fool heard what they said, and, as he was very desirous to get the red coat and cap, he saw that he must go. So he got down from by the stove, and began to put on his shoes and stockings, and to dress himself. When he was ready he took the buckets and the axe, and went down to the river, which ran near their village. When he arrived there, he cut an enormous hole in the ice. He then

drew water in the buckets, and, setting them on the
ice, he stood by the hole, looking into the water.
As he looked he saw a large pike swimming about
in the open water. Fool as Emelyan was he felt
a wish to catch this pike. So he stole on softly and
cautiously to the edge of the hole, and, making a
sudden grasp at the pike, he caught him, and pulled
him out of the water. Putting him in his bosom,
he was hurrying home, when the pike cried out—

"Ho, fool! why have you caught me?"

"To take you home," answered he, "to get my
sisters-in-law to cook you."

"Ho, fool!" said the pike; "do not take me
home, but let me go again into the water, and I
will make a rich man of you."

Emelyan, however, would not consent, and was
going on homewards. When the pike clearly saw
that the fool was not inclined to let him go, he
said—

"Hark ye, fool! let me go, and I will do for you
everything you do not like to do for yourself. You
will only have to wish, and it will be done."

When the fool heard that he rejoiced very much,
for, as he was uncommonly lazy, he thought to himself—

"If the pike does everything that I have no mind
to do, all will be done without my having any
occasion to work."

So he said to the pike—

"I will let you go in the water if you will do all you promise."

"Let me go first," said the pike, "and then I will keep my promise."

The fool, however, said that the pike must first perform his promise, and then he would let him go. When the pike saw he would not put him into the water, he said—

"If you wish, as I told you, that I should do all you desire, you must tell me now what your desire is."

"I wish," said the fool, "that my buckets should go of themselves from the river up the hill, and that without spilling any of the water."

Then said the pike—

"Remember the words I now say, and listen to what they are : 'At the pike's command, and at my request, go, buckets, of yourselves up the hill.'"

The fool repeated after him—

"At the pike's command, and at my request, go, buckets, of yourselves up the hill."

Instantly, with the speed of thought, the buckets ran up the hill. When Emelyan saw that, he was amazed beyond expression, and he said to the pike—

"But will it always be so ?"

"Everything you desire will be done," said the pike ; "but do not forget, I say, the words I have taught you."

Emelyan then put the pike into the water, and followed his buckets home.

The neighbours were all amazed when they saw
the buckets, and said to one another—

"This fool makes the buckets come of themselves
up from the river, and he follows them himself at
his leisure."

But Emelyan took no notice of them, and went on
home. The buckets were by this time in the house,
and standing in their place on the foot-bench, and
Emelyan himself lay down on the stove.

After some time his sisters-in-law said to him
again—

"Emelyan, what are you loitering there for?
Get up and cut wood."

But the fool said—

"Ay! and you! who are you, then?"

"You see," cried they, "it is now winter, and if
you do not go and cut wood you will be frozen."

"I am lazy," said the fool.

"What! you are lazy!" said the sisters-in-law.
"If you do not get up and cleave wood, we will tell
our husbands not to give you the red coat, or the
red cap, or the fine red boots." The fool, who longed
for the red cap, coat, and boots, saw that he must
cleave the wood; but as it was bitter cold, and he
did not like to leave the stove, he repeated, under
his breath, as he lay there : "At the pike's command,
and at my request, up, axe, and hew wood; and do
you, logs, come of yourselves into the house and lay
yourselves in the stove."

The axe instantly jumped up, ran into the yard, and began to cut up the wood, and the logs came of themselves into the house, and went and laid themselves in the stove. When the sisters-in-law saw this they wondered exceedingly, and as the axe did the work of itself whenever Emelyan was wanted to cut up wood, he lived with them for some time in great tranquillity. At length the wood was cut, and they said to him—

"Emelyan, we have no more wood, so you must go to the forest to cut some."

"Ay," said the fool, "and you! who are you, then?"

"The wood," said the sisters-in-law, "is far off, and it is winter, and too cold for us to go."

"I am lazy," said the fool.

"How! you are lazy!" said they, "you will be frozen, then, and besides, when our husbands come home we will tell them not to give you the red coat, cap, and boots."

As the fool longed for the red clothes, he found that he must go and cut the wood. So he got off the stove, and began to put on his shoes and stockings, and to dress himself. When he was dressed, he went out into the yard, pulled the sledge out of the shed, took a rope and the axe with him, mounted the sledge, and called out to his sisters-in-law—

"Open the gate!"

When the sisters-in-law saw that he was going

off in the sledge without any horses, for the fool
had not put the horses to it, they cried out—

" Why, Emelyan, you have got on the sledge
without yoking the horses ! "

· He answered that he did not want any horses, but
asked them to open the gate.   The sisters-in-law
threw open the gate, and the fool, as he sat in the
sledge, said—

" At the pike's command, and at my request, away,
sledge, go to the wood."

At these words the sledge galloped out of the
yard at such a rate that the people of the village,
when they saw it, were filled with amazement.
The sledge went on so very fast, that if a pair of
horses had been yoked to it they could not have
drawn it at anything like the same rate.

As it was necessary for the fool to go through the
town on his way to the wood, he came to it at full
speed.   Not knowing that he should cry out
" Make way ! " in order that he might not run over
any one, he gave no notice, but rode on.   So he
ran over a great many people ; and though they ran
after him, no one was able to overtake him and
bring him back.   Emelyan, having got clear of the
town, came to the wood, and stopped his sledge.
He then got down, and said—

" At the pike's command, and at my request, up,
axe, hew wood ; and you, logs, lay yourselves on the
sledge, and tie yourselves together."

The fool had scarcely uttered these words, when the axe began to cut wood, the logs to lay themselves in the sledge, and the rope to tie them down. When the axe had cut wood enough, he desired it to cut him a good cudgel, and when the axe had done this he mounted the sledge, and said—

"Up and away! At the pike's command, and at my request, go home, sledge."

Away went the sledge at the top of its speed. When Emelyan came to the town where he had hurt so many people, he found a crowd waiting to catch him, and as soon as he got into the town they laid hold of him, and began to drag him off his sledge and to beat him. When the fool saw how they were treating him, he said under his breath—

"At the pike's command, and at my request, up, cudgel, and thrash them."

Instantly the cudgel began to lay about it in all directions, and when the people were all driven away he made his escape, and came to his own village. The cudgel, having thrashed them all soundly, rolled to the house after him, and Emelyan, as usual when he got home, lay down on the stove.

After he had left the town the people began everywhere to talk, not about the number of persons whom he had injured, but about the amazing fact of his riding in the sledge without horses; and from one to another the news spread till it reached the court, and came even to the ears of the king. When

the king heard the story he felt an extreme desire
to see Emelyan, so he despatched an officer with a
party of soldiers in search of him. The officer
whom the king sent lost no time in leaving the
town, and he took the road that the fool had taken.
When he came to the village where Emelyan lived,
he summoned before him the Starosta (Head-man)
of the village, and said to him—

"I am sent by the king to take a certain fool, and
bring him before his majesty."

The Starosta at once showed him the house where
Emelyan lived, and the officer, entering it, asked
where the fool was. Emelyan, who was lying on
the stove, made answer and said—

"What is it you want with me ?"

"How!" said the officer. "What do I want
with you ? Get up and dress yourself. I must take
you to the king."

"What to do ?" asked Emelyan.

The officer was so enraged at the rudeness of his
replies, that he gave him a slap on the cheek.

"At the pike's command, and at my request," said
the fool, under his breath, "up, cudgel, and thrash
them."

At the word, up sprang the cudgel, and began to
lay about it on all sides, on officer and on men alike.
The officer was forced to go back to town as fast as
he could; and when he came before the king, and
told him how the fool had cudgelled them all round,

the king marvelled greatly, and would not believe that he had been able to cudgel them at all.

The king then selected a wise man, commanding him to bring him the fool by craft, if nothing else would do. The envoy left the king, and went to the village where Emelyan lived. He called the Starosta before him, and said—

"I am sent by the king to take your fool. So do you send for those with whom he lives."

The Starosta then ran and fetched the sisters-in-law. The king's messenger asked them what it was the fool liked, and they answered—

"Noble sir, if any one entreats our fool earnestly to do anything, he flatly refuses the first and the second time. The third time, however, he does not refuse, but does what one wants, for he does not like to be roughly handled."

The king's messenger then dismissed them, charging them not to tell Emelyan that he had summoned them before him. He then bought raisins, baked plums, and grapes, and went to the fool. When he came into the room, he went up to the stove, and said—

"Emelyan, why are you lying there?" and with that he gave him the raisins, baked plums, and grapes, and said—

"Emelyan, we will go together to the king. I will take you with me."

"I am very warm here," said the fool, for there was nothing he was so fond of as warmth.

The messenger then began to entreat him.

"Be so good, Emelyan," said he; "let us go. You will like the court vastly."

"Ay," said the fool; "I am lazy."

The messenger began once more to entreat him.

"Be so good," said he; "come with me, and the king will get you made a fine red coat, a red cap, and a pair of red boots."

When the fool heard the red coat mentioned, he said—

"Go on before, I will follow."

The messenger then pressed him no further, but went out and asked the sisters-in-law if there was any danger of the fool's deceiving him. They assured him that there was not, and he went his way. The fool, who was still lying on the stove, then said to himself—

"How I hate this going to the king!"

Then after a few minutes' thought—

"At the pike's command, and at my request," said he, "up stove, and away to the town."

Instantly the wall of the room opened, and the stove moved out. When it had got clear of the yard, it went at such a rate that there was no overtaking it, and it came up with the king's messenger, and went after him, and entered the palace with him. When the king knew the fool had come, he went forth with all his ministers to see him, and when he saw that Emelyan was come riding on the stove, he was greatly amazed. Emelyan still lay where he was, and said nothing. Then the king asked him why he had hurt so many people when he went to the wood.

"It was their own fault," said the fool; "why did they not get out of the way?"

Just at that moment the king's daughter came to the window and looked at the fool, and Emelyan, happening suddenly to look up at the window where she stood observing him, and seeing that she was very handsome, said, quite softly to himself—

"At the pike's command, and at my request, let this lovely maiden fall in love with me."

Scarcely had he spoken the words, when the king's daughter was desperately in love with him. He then said—

"At the pike's command, and at my request, up and away, stove, go home."

Immediately the stove left the palace, went through the town, got home, and set itself in its old place. There Emelyan lived for some time, comfortable and happy.

Other people in the town, however, were far otherwise. At the word of Emelyan the king's daughter had fallen in love with him, and she began to implore her father to give her the fool for a husband. The king was in a great rage, both with her and the fool, but he knew not how he could lay hold of him. His minister, however, suggested that he should

again send the officer whom he had before sent to
take him. This advice pleased the king well, and
he had the officer called to him. When he came the
king said—

"Hark ye, friend! I sent you before for the fool,
and you came without him. To punish you I now
send you for him a second time. If you bring him
you shall be rewarded, but if you do not bring him
you shall be punished."

When the officer heard that, he left the king, and
lost no time in going in quest of the fool. When
he came to the village, he called for the Starosta,
and said to him—

"Here is money for you. Buy everything for a
good dinner to-morrow. Invite Emelyan, and when
he comes make him drink till he falls asleep."

The Starosta, knowing that the officer came from
the king, felt obliged to obey him, so he bought
everything that was required, and invited the fool.
When Emelyan said he would come, the officer was
greatly pleased. So next day the fool came to
dinner, and the Starosta plied him so well with
drink that he fell fast asleep. As soon as the officer
saw he was asleep, he laid hold of him, and ordered
a carriage to be brought. When it came, they put
the fool in it, and the officer, getting in himself,
drove off to the town, and so to the palace. The
minister informed the king that the officer had come,
and as soon as he heard it, he ordered a large cask

to be provided without delay, and to be hooped with strong iron hoops. When the cask was brought to the king, and he saw that everything had been done as he desired, he ordered his daughter and the fool to be put into it and the cask to be well pitched. When all this had been done, the king ordered the cask to be thrown into the sea, and left to the mercy of the waves. The king then returned to his palace, and the cask floated along for some time on the sea. All this time the fool was fast asleep. When he awoke, and found it was quite dark, he said to himself—

"Where am I?" for he thought he was all alone; but the princess said—

"You are in a cask, Emelyan, and I am shut up with you in it."

"But who are you?" asked he.

"I am the king's daughter," answered the princess; and then she told him why she had been shut up there with him. She then besought him to deliver himself and her out of the cask, but the fool said—

"I am very warm here."

"Grant me the favour," said the princess; "have pity on my tears, and deliver me out of this cask."

"Why," said Emelyan; "I am lazy."

The princess began once more to entreat him.

"Grant me the favour, Emelyan," said she; "deliver me out of this cask, and let me not die."

The fool was moved by her tears and entreaties, and said—

"Well, I will do this for you."

He then said softly—

"At the pike's command, and at my request, cast us, O sea, on the shore, where we may dwell on a dry place, only let us be near our own country, and do thou, cask, fall to pieces on the dry land."

Scarcely had the fool spoken the words, when the waves began to roll, and the cask was thrown up on a dry place and fell to pieces of itself. Emelyan got up and went with the princess about the place where they were cast. The fool saw that they were in a very fine island, where there was an abundance of trees, with all kinds of fruit on them. When the princess saw that, she rejoiced greatly at their being on such an island, and she said—

"But, Emelyan, where shall we live? there is not even a nook here."

"You want too much," said the fool.

"Grant me the favour," said the princess; "let there be, if nothing more, a little cottage in which we may shelter us from the rain"—for the princess knew he could do anything he wished.

"I am lazy," said the fool.

The princess began again to urge him, and Emelyan, overcome by her entreaties, was obliged to do as she desired.

He went away from her, and said—

"At the pike's command, and at my request, let me have, in the middle of this island, a finer castle than the king's, and let a crystal bridge lead from my castle to the royal palace, and let there be people of all conditions in the court."

The words were scarcely spoken than there appeared a splendid castle with a crystal bridge. The fool went with the princess into the castle, and saw that the apartments were all magnificently furnished, and that there were many people there, such as footmen, and all kinds of officers, who waited for the fool's commands. When he saw that all these men were like men, and that he alone was ugly and stupid, he wished to be better, so he said—

"At the pike's command, and at my request, let me become such a youth that I shall have no equal, and let me be extremely wise."

He had scarcely spoken the words before he became so handsome and so wise that all were amazed.

Emelyan then sent one of his servants to the king to invite him and all his ministers to the castle. The servant went along the bridge which the fool had made, and when he came to the court the ministers brought him before the king, and Emelyan's messenger said—

"Please your majesty, I am sent by my master to ask you to dinner."

The king asked him who his master was, but he answered—

"Please your majesty, I can tell you nothing about my master, but if you come to dine with him he will inform you himself."

The king, who was curious to know who it was who had sent to invite him, told the messenger that he would come without fail.

The servant went away, and when he got home the king and his ministers set out along the crystal bridge to visit the fool. When they arrived at the castle, Emelyan came forth to meet the king, took him by the white hands, kissed him on the mouth, led him into his castle, and made him sit behind the oak tables, with fine diapered table-cloths, at sugar-meats and honey-drinks. The king and his ministers ate and drank, and made themselves merry. When they got up from table and retired, the fool said to the king—

"Does your majesty know who I am?"

As Emelyan was now dressed in fine clothes, and was very handsome, it was not possible to recognise him; so the king said that he did not know him. Then said the fool—

"Does not your majesty recollect how a fool came on a stove to your court, and how you fastened him up in a pitched cask with your daughter, and cast them into the sea? Know me then now, for I am that Emelyan."

When the king saw him thus before him, he was greatly terrified, and knew not what to do. But the fool went to the king's daughter, and brought her out to him. When the king saw her he was very pleased, and said—

"I have been very unjust towards you, so I give you my daughter for your wife."

Hearing that, Emelyan thanked the king, and when he had prepared everything for the wedding, it was celebrated with great magnificence, and the following day Emelyan gave a feast to the ministers and to the common people. There were barrels of wine set forth; and when all these festivities were at an end, the king wanted to give up his kingdom to him, but Emelyan had no mind to take it. So the king went back to his kingdom, and Emelyan remained in his castle, and lived happily.

ILIJA, THE MUROMER.

In the celebrated city of Murom, near to Katat-scharowa, there lived a countryman named Ivan Timofejevitch. He had one son named Ilija, the Muromer, and of him he was very fond. He was thirty years old when he began to walk. Then, all of a sudden, not only did he become strong enough to go about, but also made himself a suit of armour and a steel spear. Then he saddled his horse, went to his father and mother, and asked them for their blessing, saying—

"Father and mother of mine, let me go to the celebrated town of Kiev, to pray to God and to see the prince."

His father and mother gave him their blessing, and said to him—

"Go, then, to the town of Kiev, to the town of Tschernigof, and do no wrong on your way, and spill no Christian blood wantonly."

Ilija, the Muromer, received their blessing, and prayed to God. Then he bid his parents farewell, and went on his way. He travelled so far in a dark forest that at length he came to the hold of some robbers. As soon as the robbers saw the Muromer, they began to wish for his beautiful horse, and they said one to another—

"Let us seize this horse, which is so beautiful that its like has never been seen, and let us take it from this unknown fellow."

So they all, five-and-twenty, set upon Ilija, the Muromer. Ilija reined in his horse, took an arrow out of his quiver, put it on the string of his bow, and shot it into the ground with so much force that the pieces of earth flew over three acres. When the robbers saw that they looked at one another with astonishment. Then they threw themselves on their knees, and said—

"Master and father, we have wronged you. If you want to punish us take our treasure, our fine clothes, and as many of our horses as you like."

"What should I do with your treasure?" said Ilija. "If you want to keep your lives, see that you do not do the like in future." So he went on to famous Kiev. He came at length to the town of Tschernigof, and found it beset by an army of pagans, so great that no one could tell their number. They wanted to destroy the town, tear down the churches, and carry off the princes and nobles as slaves. When Ilija, the Muromer, saw the army he was afraid, but he placed confidence in the Highest, and braced himself up to die for the Christian

religion.   So he attacked the pagan army, put them
to flight, took the chiefs prisoners, and carried them
to Tschernigof.   When he came to the city the
folk ran out to meet him, the prince and the nobles
coming first.   They gave him thanks, and then went
with him to offer up praise to God, who had pre-
served the town safe, and not allowed it to be
overthrown by so large an army.

Then they conducted Ilija to the palace, and entertained him at a great feast.   After that Ilija, the
Muromer, went straight on to Kiev, along a road
which the Robber Nightingale had kept for thirty
years, and on which he suffered no horseman or
traveller on foot to pass, putting them to death, not
by the sword, but by the sound of his robber whistle.
When Ilija came into the open fields he rode on to
the Bianski forest, and went far on, passing over
marshes, by means of bridges made of water-elder, to
the river Smarodienka.   When the Robber Nightingale saw him about twenty versts away, he guessed
his errand, and sounded his robber whistle.   But the
hero did not quail, and came on till he was only ten
versts off, when the robber blew his whistle so loudly
that Ilija's horse fell down on its knees.   Then Ilija
went up to the robber's nest, which was built upon
twelve oaks.   When the robber saw the hero he
blew with all his might and tried to kill him, but
Ilija took his bow, put a new arrow on the string,
shot it straight into the robber's nest, and hit the

robber in the right eye. Robber Nightingale fell down from the tree like a sheaf of oats.

Ilija, the Muromer, took him, bound him fast to his saddle, and rode away to Kiev. At the side of the road stood the palace of Robber Nightingale, and as he rode by the robber's daughters were sitting at the open window.

"There comes our father," said the youngest, "riding, and bringing with him a peasant, tied to his saddle."

The eldest looked at him carefully, and began to weep bitterly.

"It is not our father," said she, "that rides there, but a strange man who has made him prisoner."

Then they called out to their husbands—

"Dear husbands, ride out against this stranger, and deliver our father from him. Let not such shame come on us!"

Their husbands were mighty riders, and they came out to attack the Russian horseman; and they had good horses and sharp lances, and thought it would be an easy matter to kill him. When Robber Nightingale saw them, he called out and said—

"My dear sons, let no shame come on you, and do not attack so brave a knight, for if you do he will but slay you. Ask him, rather, to enter the house and drink with us."

When Ilija heard the invitation he turned to

enter the palace, suspecting no treachery; but the
eldest daughter had hung a beam, by means of a
chain, over the entrance, so that she might kill him
as he rode through. When Ilija saw that he gave
her a stroke with his lance and killed her. Then
he rode on to Kiev and came to the prince's palace.
He entered the palace, prayed to God, and saluted
the nobles.

"Tell me, my good young man," said the prince,
"what is your name, and to what place you
belong ? "

"I am called Little Ilija, sir," said he; "my father
is Ivan, and I was born in the town of Murom,
near to Katatscharowa."

The prince next asked him by what road he had
come.

"From Murom I rode to Tschernigof, and there I
slew a great host of pagans and saved the city.
From that place I came here. I have taken prisoner
the famous Robber Nightingale, and I have brought
him here bound to my stirrup."

Then the prince grew angry, and said—

"Why do you try to deceive me ? "

However, he sent two knights, Alescha Popo-
witsch and Dobrinja Nikititsch, to see if it was as
Ilija said; and when they told the prince that it was
true, he was pleased, gave the young man some
drink, and desired to hear the robber's whistle.
Ilija, the Muromer, therefore wrapped up the prince

and the princess under his cloak, lined with sable, put them under his arm, and then told the Robber Nightingale to blow his whistle gently. He blew, however, so loud that he deafened all the knights and they fell on the floor, and Ilija, the Muromer, was so enraged that he killed him there and then.

Ilija became very friendly with Dobrinja Nikititsch, and, saddling their good horses, they rode away together, and travelled for three months without meeting with any adversary. Then they came up with a cripple. His beggar's cloak weighed fifty pounds, his hat nine pounds, and his crutch was six feet long. Ilija, the Muromer, rode up to him and began to try his courage, but the cripple addressing him said—

"Ah! Ilija, the Muromer, do you not know me? Do you not remember how we learnt lessons in the same school? Will you fall on me, a poor cripple? Do you know that there is great distress in the famous town of Kiev? A powerful infidel knight, a godless idolater, has come there. His head is as big as a beer-barrel, his eyebrows are a span apart, and his shoulders are six feet across. He eats an ox at a meal, and drinks a cask of beer at a time. The Prince is sore troubled at your absence."

Then Ilija, the Muromer, put on the cripple's cloak and rode off to Kiev. He went to the palace, and cried with all his might—

"Ho, there! Prince of Kiev, give the cripple an alms."

When the Prince heard him, he said—

"Come into my palace. I will give you something to eat and drink, and some money for your journey."

Then Ilija went into the palace and sat down near the stove, and there also sat the pagan knight calling for food to be brought. The servants brought him an ox, roasted whole, and he ate it up, bones and all. Then he called for something to drink, and twenty-seven men brought him a barrel of beer. The knight took it in his hands and lifted it up. Then Ilija, the Muromer, said—

"My father once had a gluttonous mare, which ate so much that it burst."

The infidel was angry, and said—

"What do you mean, you wretched cripple? You are no equal for me. I could set you on the palm of my right hand and squeeze you dry with my left. You once had a real hero in your country, Ilija, the Muromer; I should like to have a fight with him."

"Here he is," cried Ilija, taking off his hat, and striking the pagan a blow on the head, not very hard, but so strong as to send the head through the wall of the palace. Ilija then took up the body and cast it into the yard. So the prince gave Ilija a royal reward, and kept him at his court as the first and the bravest of his knights.

THE BAD-TEMPERED WIFE.

THERE was once upon a time a poor fellow who was troubled with a wife, with whom he lived on the worst terms imaginable. She paid not the slightest attention to what he told her, but was always contrary. If he told her to get up early, she was sure to lie in bed later than ever, or perhaps even for three days at a time. If he asked her to make some cakes, she would say—

"Cakes, you villain! What do you want with cakes? Do you think you deserve them?"

"All right," the man would say; "don't make them, then."

Then off would go his wife, make three times as many cakes as could be eaten, and plumping them down before her husband—

"Eat," she would cry—"eat, you gluttonous fellow! They must be finished up."

The man spent most of his time disputing with her; but his wife used to wear him out and get the better in the end.

One day, wearied by his wife's jangle, and utterly dispirited, he went off to the wood to look for some

berries. As he went on he came at last to a wild
currant-bush, and looking at it he saw beside it a
deep hole. He looked down, but could discover no
bottom to it.

"Dear me!" said he, "I wish my wife were
down there! What is the use of living as I do in
continual misery? I will see if I can get her down
the hole."

Off he went home. There he found his wife.

"Wife," said he, "I want you to. keep out of the
wood. Don't go looking about there for berries."

"You want me!" said she. "Indeed, I shall go
where I please."

"Well," said the man, "I have found a currant-
bush there, and I want to keep the currants. Don't
eat them."

"Won't I?" said his wife. "I will eat them all.
You shall not have a single one."

The man went out, and his wife came after him
to find the currant-bush. On they went till the
man came to the place where the bush was, when
his wife, hurrying past him, got to it first.

"Now don't you come near," said she. "I warn
you to stand off."

On she went; all at once her husband heard a
crack and a crash. He looked about, but could not
see his wife. Sure enough, she had fallen down the
hole.

The man returned home rejoicing at the success

of his plan. For some days he lived in peace. Then he became curious to know where his wife had really gone to. So he got a very long cord, and set off with it to the forest. He came to the currant-bush and found the hole, and, letting down one end of his cord, tried to touch the bottom. The cord went down and down—the hole seemed to have no bottom at all. Then the man drew the cord up. As he pulled out the last piece of it, he fell back astounded, for there, clinging to it, was a little devil. After the first surprise, the man was about to lay his hands on the imp in order to throw him down the hole again; but it addressed him in a pitiful tone, saying—

"My good man, I beseech you do not throw me down the hole again. No tongue can tell what I have suffered there. A few days since there came a woman amongst us, and she has led us such a time of it that our lives are not worth living. Let me stay aboveground, and I will reward you for it."

The peasant, when he heard the imp's tale, felt sorry for him, and had not the heart to send him back again. So he let him go where he would.

No sooner was the imp at liberty than he began to torment the wives and daughters of the wealthy folk, entering into them, and making them so whimsical and sick that they seemed beside themselves. While they were in this condition the peasant would present himself as a physician and undertake to cure the afflicted persons. As soon as he was called in, before he had almost stepped across the threshold of the house in which the sick person lay, the imp would scuttle away as fast as he could, the patient recovered, and the whole place rang with the marvellous cure effected by the doctor. So they went on for some time. The peasant was now rich. Money and all good things were heaped upon him by the relations of those whom he restored to health.

One day the imp said to him—

"My man, I have had enough of this kind of thing. I am now going to take possession of a rich man's daughter. Don't you come to heal her, for I warn you that if you do so I will tear you to pieces."

Away he went. The daughter was possessed, and was so beside herself that no one dare venture near her. Away sent her relations for the wonderful doctor. The peasant, however, was unwilling to take the case in hand. He would not come. At last the folk sent their servants to bring him to the house by force, declaring that if he refused to come they would kill him.

The man did not know what to do; at last he thought he saw his way out of the difficulty.

In the road running beside the house he collected a number of coachmen, grooms, and others, and ordered them to run up and down, smacking their whips and crying as loudly as they could—

"That wretched woman has come again! that wretched woman has come again!"

When the hubbub was at its full height the peasant went into the house.

"What!" cried the imp. "You have come, have you? Well then, now, I will make you repent it."

"My dear friend," said the man, "it is true I have come, but I came to do you a service. I came to tell you that that miserable woman has come back again."

"What!" cried the imp.

He leaped to the window, looked out, and listened. When he saw the confusion, and heard the cries—"That wretched woman has come again! that wretched woman has come again!" he turned to the peasant, and said to him, in a tone full of anxiety and mournfulness—

"What shall I do? Where can I hide from her?"

"I don't know," said the man, "but I should say the hole would be the safest place. She will hardly search there a second time for you."

Away went the imp at full speed, and, coming to the hole, down he went headlong. He was never seen again. The girl was completely cured when he left her, and was as happy as ever, and her parents heaped rewards on the wonderful physician.

The bad-tempered woman, too, never made her appearance again, so it seems as if she would remain down the pit for ever.

IVASHKA WITH THE BEAR'S EAR.

ONCE upon a time there lived in a certain kingdom a moujik. He was married, and his wife bore him a child—a boy—who had the ear of a bear, so he was named Ivashka with the Bear's Ear. Ivashka used to go and play with the children of his neighbours, but his manner was rather rough, for if he took hold of a child by the hand he would give it such a wrench that the hand would come off, and if he took hold of a child by the head, the head would come off too. Such play was not agreeable to the parents of the children, and they came to Ivashka's father and told him that he must see that his son did not come out to play with their children, or that he did them no hurt. The man promised to do what he could. He found, however, that Ivashka paid no heed to him, so in the end he turned him out of doors, saying—

" Be off where you will, for I want you no longer ; you shall come no more into my house, for if you do you will get me into trouble."

So Ivashka with the Bear's Ear set off on his

travels. He went on for a long time, and at last
came to a great forest. There he found a man
hewing wood.

"Friend," said Ivashka to him, "what are you
called?"

"I am called Dubunia," said the man.

"Well," said Ivashka, "let us be friends."

After some talk they became very friendly, and
the man went on with Ivashka. They travelled for
some time, and at length they came to a high rock,
where they found a man hewing stone.

"Heaven bless you, good fellow!" said Ivashka;
"what are you called?"

"Gorunia," replied the man.

"Well," said Ivashka, "let us be friends."

After some talk the man became very friendly
with Ivashka and his companion, and agreed to go
on with them in their travels. On they went. At
last they came to a river, on the bank of which they
found a man with very long moustaches, with which
he was fishing in the water.

"Heaven bless you!" said Ivashka and his companions. "May you have good luck."

"Thanks, my brothers," said the man.

"What are you called?" asked Ivashka.

"Usunia," said he.

"Well," said Ivashka, "let us be friends."

So, after some talk, the man agreed to join
Ivashka and his companions.

The four went on, and at length they came to a forest, near to which they found a hut. Now the hut stood on a fowl's legs, and kept turning round and round.

"Hut, hut," cried Ivashka, "stand still with your back to the forest and your front towards us!"

The hut at once did what they told it, and the four travellers going in commenced to plan how they should live. They were very hungry, so they went into the forest, caught some game, and ate it.

The next day Dubunia stayed at home while the others went into the forest to look for game. He cooked the dinner, and waited for his companions to come back. They did not come, so Dubunia washed his head and sat combing his hair, and who should come into the hut but Baba Yaja. She came riding in an iron mortar, which she drove on with a pestle, and with her tongue she wiped out the marks the mortar made as it passed over the ground. As she came into the cabin—

"Ho, ho!" cried she, "I smell Russian flesh."

Then she turned to Dubunia and said—

"What do you do here?"

Without waiting for his reply, Baba Yaja laid on him with her pestle, and beat him until he hardly had any life left in him. Then she ate the dinner he had got ready for his companions, got into her mortar, and rode off. Dubunia lay for some time on the ground. Then he got up, tied up his head with a handkerchief, and sat down, groaning, till his companions came home.

" Where is the dinner ? " said they.

"I have been ill," answered Dubunia, and have been too unwell to get it ready."

The next day Gorunia was left to keep the hut and get the dinner ready. He cooked the food, and waited for his friends to come back, when, all of a sudden, who should come in but Baba Yaja.

" Ho, ho ! " said she, "I smell Russian flesh. What are you doing here ? " she asked, turning to Gorunia.

Without giving him time to reply she commenced to beat him with the pestle. Then she ate up all the food he had ready, got into the mortar, and rode away. When his friends came home Gorunia told them what had happened.

On the third day Usunia stayed at home, and Baba Yaja made her appearance again, and treated him as she had his companions.

At length it was Ivashka's turn to keep house. His comrades went out to hunt in the wood, and Ivashka got the dinner ready. Looking about the hut he found in it a jar of honey. Then Ivashka took an axe and split open one of the posts of the hut, and putting a piece of wood in at the top he kept the crack open. Then he took the honey and poured it all over the post and in the chink. After that he got three iron rods, and then he sat down

to await Baba Yaja's coming. He did not wait
long, for she came riding to the hut in her mortar.

"Ho, ho!" cried she, as she entered, "I smell
Russian flesh. What do you here?" said she,
turning to Ivashka.

Just then, however, she smelt the honey, and,
going to the post, she commenced to lick it with her
long tongue. She licked all the honey off the
outside, and then put her tongue in the crack, to get
the honey out that was there. Then Ivashka
suddenly pulled out the piece of wood that held
the post asunder, and Baba Yaja's tongue being held
fast, she could not get away. She screamed and
struggled, but could not free herself, and Ivashka,
taking his three iron rods, commenced to beat her
with all his strength. He beat her till he was tired;
and then, as she begged him to have mercy on her,
and promised that if he would let her go she would
never trouble him more, he set her free.

"Stop there," said he, putting her in a corner of
the cabin. So he sat down and waited for his
companions to come home. Towards evening they
came, and how much were they surprised to find
that Ivashka had the food cooked and ready for
them! When they had eaten he told them how he
had served Baba Yaja, and how he had beaten her and
put her in the corner of the hut. When they went
to look for her, however, she was nowhere to be
seen. While they examined the place to find how

she could have escaped, they discovered a large stone
in the ground. Lifting it up they found there was
a deep pit below. They wished very much to know
what was in this place, but none durst go down, till
Ivashka said he would go. So they made a rope
and let him down.

"Wait for me," said Ivashka; "but if I do not
come back at the end of a week, know then that
you will see me no more. When I want to come
up I will pull the rope." So he took leave of his
companions, and they let him down. When he
arrived at the bottom of the pit he found himself
in a strange country. He went on for some time
until he came to a hut, and, going in, he found three
girls who sat sewing with gold thread.

"What do you want?" said they, when they saw
Ivashka with the Bear's Ear. "What has brought
you here? Baba Yaja, our mother, lives here, and
if she sees you she will certainly kill you. We will,
however, tell you how you may save your life if you
will take us to the upper world."

Ivashka promised to do what they asked.

"When our mother comes in," said they, "she will
run at you and attack you. When you have fought for
a time she will leave you and go to the cellar. There
are two jars full of water: the one is white and
the other is blue. The white jar contains the water
of weakness, and the blue jar the water of strength.
If you drink the water in the blue jar you are saved."

The girls had scarcely finished speaking when Baba Yaja was heard coming to the hut. She came riding in the iron mortar, which she drove along with the pestle, while, with her tongue, she swept out the mark made by the mortar as it passed over the ground.

"Ho, ho!" said she, "I smell Russian flesh. Why do you come here?" she went on, turning to Ivashka with the Bear's Ear. "What do you want?"

With that she rushed upon him, and they fought together until they were so tired that they fell to the ground. Then Baba Yaja, getting up, ran to the cellar for the water, and Ivashka went after her. Baba Yaja, in her hurry, took up the white jar and drank the water, and Ivashka drank that in the blue jar. Then they began to fight again. At length Ivashka got the better of her, and taking her pestle he beat her with it till she begged him to have mercy on her. Still Ivashka would not stop till she promised him she would never do him any injury, and would leave that place as soon as he released her. So he let her go.

Ivashka went to the three daughters and told them to get ready and go with him to the world above. Then he went to the rope, and, calling to his companions, got them to let down a large basket. He told the eldest daughter to get into it, and then, on Ivashka's pulling the rope, his companions drew the basket up. They were very much astonished when they found a beautiful girl in the basket instead of Ivashka, but she told them all that had occurred, and they let the basket down again. So the second and the third daughters were drawn up. Then they let down the basket again, and Ivashka filled it with gold and silver and fine clothes, which he had found in Baba Yaja's hut. When the men commenced to draw the basket up they wondered why it was so heavy, and they thought that Baba Yaja herself must be in it. So they cut the rope and let the basket and all the things fall down to the bottom, and left Ivashka down below.

For a long time he wandered about seeking his way to the upper world. At length he found an iron door in the rock, and on opening it and looking in he saw a long passage. So he went on and on till at last he came out in the upper world. Then he went to seek his friends. When he came to them he found that they had given him up as dead, and had married the three daughters of Baba Yaja.

"Why did you leave me at the bottom of the pit?" asked Ivashka; "and who was it that cut the rope?"

They told him that Usunia had done it, and Ivashka was so angry that he killed him on the spot. So Ivashka married Usunia's wife, and he and his companions lived together for many years in great happiness.

THE PLAGUE.

A RUSSIAN peasant sat out in the field. The sun was shining fiercely. In the distance the man saw something coming to him. It came nearer, and then he saw it was a woman. She was clad in a large cloak, and strode along with great strides. The man felt much afraid, and would have run away, but the phantom held him with its bare arms.

"Do you know the Plague?" said she. "I am it. Take me on your shoulders and carry me through all Russia. Miss no village or town, for I must go everywhere. For yourself fear nothing. You shall live in the midst of death."

She wrapt her long arms round the neck of the fearful peasant. The man went on, and was astonished to find that he felt no weight. He turned his head, and saw that the Plague was on his back.

He first took her to a town, and when they came there there was joy in all the streets, dancing, music, and jollity. The peasant went on and stood in the market-place, and the woman shook her cloak. Soon the dance, joy, and merriment ceased.

Wherever the man looked he saw terror. People carried coffins, the bells tolled, the burial-ground was full; there was at length no room for more to be buried in it.

Then the people brought the dead to the market-place and left them there, having no place in which to bury them.

The wretched man went on. Whenever he came to a village the houses were left deserted, and the peasants fled with white faces, and trembling with fear. On the roads, in the woods, and out in the fields, could be heard the groans of the dying.

Upon a high hill stood the man's own village, the place in which he was born, and to this place the Plague began to direct his steps. There were the man's wife, his children, and his old parents.

The man's heart was bleeding! When he came near his own village, he laid hold of the Plague so that she should not escape him, and held her with all his might.

He looked before him and saw the blue Pruth flowing past, and beyond it were the green hills, and afar off the dark mountains with snow-capped tops.

He ran quickly to the stream and leaped under its waters, wishing to destroy himself and his burden together, and so free his land from sorrow and the Plague.

He himself was drowned, but the Plague, being as light as a feather, slipped off his shoulders, and so escaped. She was, however, so alarmed by this brave deed that she fled away and hid herself in the mountain forests.

So the man saved his village, his parents, his wife, and his little children, and all that part of fair Russia through which the Plague had not passed.

THE PEASANT AND THE WIND.

ONCE upon a time there was a peasant who lived in great poverty with his wife. He was as dull as a sheep, but she was as wily as a serpent, and she was so bad tempered that she used to beat him for any little thing that put her out.

One day the woman begged some corn of a neighbour so that she might make some bread, and she sent her husband off to the mill with it to get it ground. The miller knew they were very poor, so he ground the corn for nothing, and the man set off to go home with the flour. As he was on his way there came all of a sudden such a fierce blast of wind that all the flour was, in a moment, blown away out of the pan which he carried on his head. So the man went home and told his wife what had happened. When she heard his story she set upon him and gave him a hearty beating, and then, having scolded and thrashed till she could do no more, she told him to be off to the wind and ask it either to give him the flour back again or to pay him for it.

The man went off out of the house, weeping; and,

not knowing in what direction to go, he went to a great dark forest. There he wandered about, here and there. At last an old woman met him.

"Good man," said she, "where are you going? How came you in these parts, where no bird ever flies, and scarce a wild animal runs?"

"My mother," said he, "I have been forced to come here. I carried some corn to the mill to be ground, and when it was finished, as I carried the flour home, the wind came and scattered it all out of the pan. I had no flour when I got home, and I told my wife what had happened; so she beat me, and sent me off to the wind to ask it to give me the flour again or to pay me for it. So I came here to look for the wind, but I do not know where to find it."

"Come with me," said the woman. "I am the mother of the winds, and I have four sons. The first is the East-wind, the second the South-wind, the third the West-wind, and the fourth the North-wind. Tell me, now, which wind was it that took your flour?"

"It was the South-wind," said the man.

The old woman led the man deep into the forest, and bringing him to a little hut, said—

"Here we are, my man. Climb up upon the stove and cover yourself up, for my children will soon be here."

"Why should I cover myself?" asked the man.

"Because, my son, the North-wind, will be here,"

said the woman, "and he will otherwise freeze you up."

In a short time the sons began to come in. When the South-wind had arrived, the old woman told the man to come off the stove, and said to her son—

"South-wind, my dear son, this man has a complaint against you. Why do you hurt the poor? You have taken this man's flour out of his pan. Now give him money for it, or make him some recompense."

"Very well, mother," said the South-wind, "I will buy the flour of him."

So saying, he turned to the man, and said—

"Here, my man. Take this basket. It has in it all you most want—money, bread, food, and drink of all kinds. You have only to say to it, 'Basket, give me so and so,' and it will give you whatever you wish. Take it to your house. I give it you for your flour."

The peasant bowed to the Wind, thanked it for the basket, and set off homewards.

He gave the basket to his wife, and said—

"Wife, here is a basket which contains everything, whatever you most want. You only have to ask for it."

The woman took the basket, and said to it—

"Basket, give me some good flour, so that I may make bread."

The basket gave her as much as she wished.

She continued asking for very many things, and everything she named the basket gave her.

Now it chanced that one day a nobleman was passing by the peasant's hut. When the woman saw him she said to her husband—

"Go and ask the nobleman to dine with us. If you do not bring him in I will beat you till you are half dead."

The man was afraid of his wife carrying out her threat, so he set off and asked the stranger in to dinner.

His wife meanwhile watched him from the window, having taken out of the basket all that was required for the dinner. There she sat, with her hands in her lap, awaiting her husband's return with the guest.

The nobleman was astonished, and laughed at the invitation. He would not accept it himself, but told his attendants they might go if they wished, and he should like to know how they dined.

So the attendants went, thinking they should fare very badly, for the appearance of the hut would not have led any one to suppose that there was much feasting to be had within it. When they entered they were vastly astonished. The dinner was such as would have done credit had it been provided by a host of some rank. The men sat down, and ate and drank and made merry ; and, keeping their eyes open the while, they observed that when the woman wanted anything for the table she went to the basket and got it given to her by it. The men began to think how they could get the prize for themselves. As they feasted they sent off one of their number to look for a basket just like the one in the room. Off went the man as quickly as he could, found what he wanted, and brought it with him to the cottage. Then while the peasant and his wife were busy, the men slipped the new basket in the place of the other. When they left they carried away the treasure-basket with them, and coming to their master they told him how they had been entertained.

After the feast was over and the guests had gone, the peasant's wife cast away the food that was left, for what was the use of keeping it when fresh could be so easily got? The next morning she went to the basket and asked it for various things, but a great change seemed to have come over it, for it paid no heed to her.

"Old Greyhead," cried she to her husband, "this is a nice basket you have got us! What is the good of it if it does not do what we tell it? Be off to the wind again, and tell it to give you back your flour, or I will thrash you till you are half dead."

There was nothing for it but he must go. He came to the old woman's hut, and there he began to tell her what a terrible wife he had got, and the old woman told him to wait a while till her son, the South-wind, came home.

Not long after in came the South-wind, and the
peasant told him all about his trouble.

"Well," said the wind, when he had heard him
to an end, "I am sorry, old man, that you have such
a bad wife, but I will help you, and your wife shall
thrash you no more. Here now is a cask. Take
it home with you, and when your wife threatens to
beat you, stand behind the cask and say, 'Five,
come out of the cask and beat my wife!' When
you think they have punished her sufficiently, say,
'Five, go back to your cask!'"

The peasant was very grateful to the Wind, made
him his best bow, and went home. When he got
there, he said—

"There, wife, now you have a cask instead of the
basket."

His wife flew into a rage, and said—

"What do I want with your cask? Why didn't
you bring the flour with you?"

She grasped a weapon as she said this, and got
ready to lay on her husband, but he slipped behind
the cask, and when he saw how matters were, he
said—

"Five, come out of the cask and beat my wife!"

In an instant out sprang five big fellows, who
set to to thrash the wife. The husband looked on
till he thought she had had enough. Then he listened to her cries for mercy, and said—

"Five, go back to your cask!"

In the twinkling of an eye the men ceased their labour, and disappeared into the cask again. From that hour the woman was much improved, and the peasant, seeing that he should not want the cask in order to preserve quiet at home, began to think whether he could not somehow obtain his basket by means of it. He concluded that the nobleman's servants must have taken the basket away, and he and his wife set their heads together to think how they could get it from them.

"Since you have such a marvellous cask," said she, "you need not be afraid even of a thousand men. Why not then go to the nobleman and make him give you the basket." Her husband thought the idea was a good one, so he went off to the nobleman's house and asked him to come outside and fight him. He laughed at the peasant, but thought he would have a joke with him, so he told him to await him outside. Off went the peasant, took his cask under his arm, and came to the spot where the nobleman was to meet him. In a short time he came, bringing with him several of his servants. As soon as he had come up he ordered his attendants to set on the peasant and give him a good thrashing; but he, when he saw the gentleman's trickery, fell in a rage, and shouted out—

"Look you, sir, will you give me back my basket, or will you not? It shall be better for you all if you do!"

When, however, he saw that no one paid any attention to what he said, and that the attendants were about to thrash him, he cried out—

"Five to each man come out of the cask, and beat them thoroughly!"

In an instant there sprang forth five stout fellows for each of them, and they laid upon them most unmercifully. The nobleman was afraid he should be beaten till there was no life in him, and so he called out—

"Good fellow, for Heaven's sake, do not beat us any more!"

When the peasant heard that, he said—

"Go back to the cask, you fellows."

In a moment the cudgels ceased to play, and the men disappeared into the cask. The gentleman had had enough. He ordered that the basket should be given up to the peasant as quickly as possible, and the man taking it home with him, he and his wife lived very happily ever after.

THE WONDERFUL CLOTH.

THERE was once a shepherd who looked after the king's flocks. He had three sons, two of whom were considered very clever, but the third was looked upon as a fool. The elder brothers helped their father to herd the flocks, but the youngest, who was thought to be good for nothing, played about or went to sleep.

He passed his days and nights sleeping on the top of the stove, and never left that place unless he was driven from it. If he bestirred himself, it was rather because he was too hot, or wanted something to eat or drink. His father did not care for him, and called him a lazy fellow, while his brothers often tormented him, pulling him off the stove or refusing to let him eat. If his mother had not looked after him he would have been nearly starved. She, however, would caress him and give him food. Was it his fault that he was a fool? Who could tell what Heaven had in store for him? It sometimes happens that the wisest folk do not get on well, and that fools, especially such as are harmless and inoffensive, succeed in a wonderful fashion.

One day when the two brothers returned from the fields, finding the simpleton on the top of the stove, they made him dress and put on his hat, and having dragged him into the yard, they gave him a good beating, and turning him out, said to him—

"Go, simpleton, and lose no time, for you shall have neither lodging nor supper until you have gone to the wood and brought us a basket of mushrooms."

The poor fellow, full of astonishment, did not even understand what his brothers wished of him. After having stood for a time scratching his head, he set off to a little forest of oak-trees which was near at hand. All seemed wonderful and strange to him. Right in his way he came across the dry trunk of a tree. He went up to it, took off his hat, and said—

"I see that other trees in the forest stand up and wear hats of green leaves, but you alone, my poor friend, are bare. The cold will kill you. You are amongst just such brothers as I have. No doubt you are a fool like myself. Will you have my hat, then?"

Folding his arms, he wept tenderly. All of a sudden one of the trees which grew near moved as if it were alive. The idiot was alarmed, and was about to fly, when the tree, addressing him in a man's voice, said—

', Do not fly, but stop and listen. That tree,

which was cut down so prematurely, was my son. No one besides myself has until now wept over his so early blighted life. You alone have watered him with your tears. As a reward for it, you shall henceforth obtain whatever you ask of me, saying the following words :—

"Oak with the golden acorns, I beseech you give me what I want!"

At the moment that the oak ceased, a shower of golden acorns fell upon the idiot, who filled his pockets with them, saluted the oak, thanked it, and returned home.

"Ah, you simpleton!" cried his brothers, "where are the mushrooms?"

"I have in my pocket some oak mushrooms," said the idiot.

"Eat them yourself, then, for your supper," said they, "for you will have nothing else, you sluggard. Where is your hat?"

"I covered a poor tree I came across on the road with it; it had nothing on it, and I was afraid it would be frozen," answered he.

The idiot climbed upon the stove as he said this, and lay down. All of a sudden the golden acorns fell out of his pocket. The brothers rushed forward, and paying no heed to the lad's remonstrances, gathered up the acorns and took them to their father. He told them to carry them to the king, and tell him that one of his sons, an idiot, had found them in the wood. When the king saw them, he at once sent some soldiers to look through the wood for golden acorns, but all their search was fruitless. They came back and told him that there was not a single golden acorn to be found in the forest. The king fell in a great rage when he heard that. When he was calm again, he ordered the shepherd to come to him, and said—

"Tell your son, the idiot, that he must bring to the court this evening a cask full to the brim of gold acorns. If he does so he shall receive my royal favour, and you may be assured that you shall not be forgotten."

The shepherd went off to his son, and told him what the king had said.

"The king," said the idiot, "I see, likes good things. He does not ask, but commands me to do what he wishes, and makes mere promises, and for them he wants a fool to bring him golden acorns. I shall not do it."

Neither the prayers nor the threats of his father could make him change his mind. At last his brothers pulled him off the stove, made him dress and put on a hat, took him into the yard and beat him, and then put him out, saying—

"Lose no time, you simpleton, but be off, for you shall have neither lodging nor supper till you return from the wood with the golden acorns."

The fool did not know what to do, so he set off

again to the forest. In a short time he came to the stump on which was his hat, just by the old oak. He raised his cap, bowed, and said—

"Oak with the golden acorns, help me in my distress, I beseech you. Give me what I want."

The oak shook itself, rattled its branches, and instead of golden acorns a cloth fell into the lad's hands.

"Take care of the cloth," said the oak, "and keep it. In case of need, say to it—

"'Wonderful cloth, let one who is hungry and thirsty find here everything he wants.'"

The oak ceased, and the lad, saluting and thanking it, commenced to go home. As he went he wondered what his brothers would say to him, and he thought how pleased his mother would be when he told her that he had got the wonderful cloth. When he was half-way home he met a beggar, who said to him—

"See, I am old, ill, and ragged, for the love of God give me something, either money or a piece of bread."

The idiot laid his cloth on the grass, and said—

"Wonderful cloth, let those who are hungry and thirsty find here all they want."

Immediately there was a whistling in the air; something shone over them, and they found before them a table set as if for a king's feast. There were numberless dishes, goblets full of hydromel,.

and glasses full of the best wines. The things on the table were all of gold or of silver.

The idiot and his guest admired the table and commenced to eat and drink. When they had finished eating and drinking the table vanished, and the idiot wrapped up his cloth and began to go homewards, when the old man said to him—

"Give me your cloth, and take this stick in its stead. When you speak to it such-and-such words it belabours people so that they will give all the world to escape from it."

The idiot, thinking of his brothers, took the cudgel and gave the man the cloth. So they parted.

Now afterwards he considered that the oak had told him to keep the cloth himself, and that, having given it away, he would not be able to surprise his mother as he had intended. So he said to the stick—

"Stick which beats by itself, go quickly and look for my cloth. Go, I want it back."

The stick went off at once in pursuit of the man and soon overtook him. It set upon him, and commenced to beat him, crying—

"So you seek the wealth of others, do you? Take that, you knave, and that."

The man tried to escape, but it was no use, for the stick followed him, thrashing on, and repeating the same words. However much he would have liked to keep the cloth, he was obliged to throw it aside to save himself. The stick brought the cloth to its master, and the idiot continued his journey, thinking how he would surprise his mother and brothers. A little further on he met a man who carried in his hand an empty bag.

"Stop," cried the man. "For the love of Heaven give me some pence or a piece of bread! My bag is empty, and I am hungry and have a long way to go."

The fool spread his cloth once more, and said—

"Wonderful cloth, let him who is hungry and thirsty find here everything he wants."

They heard a whistling noise, saw something shine in the air above them, and, immediately, in front of them, was a table set as if for a royal banquet. There were numberless dishes, and hydromel and wine in plenty. The idiot and his guest sat down, and when they had finished eating and drinking the table disappeared. The fool wrapped up his cloth, and was commencing his journey, when the man said to him—

"Will you give me your cloth for my girdle? When you say, 'Girdle, which swims so wonderfully, for my safety and not for my pleasure, let me find myself in a boat on the water,' the girdle will change itself into a deep lake, upon which you can sail at your will."

The simpleton thought how much his father would like to always have water for his flocks. So

he gave the man the cloth for the girdle, which he
tied around him. Then he took his stick in his
hand, and the two parted. In a short time, when
the beggar was afar off, the fool began again to
remember how the oak had told him to keep the
cloth for himself, and he saw that unless he had it
he would not be able to give his mother the pleasant
surprise he had intended. So he said to his
stick—

"Stick, which beats of itself, go quickly and
look for my cloth. Go, I want it back."

The stick set off again, and coming up to the
beggar commenced to beat him, saying—

"So you seek the wealth of others, do you?
Take that, knave, and that."

The beggar tried to fly, but the stick pursued
him, and however much he would have liked to
keep the cloth, he preferred rather to save himself
from the stick. The cudgel brought the cloth to
its master, and he, having hidden it under his coat,
put on the girdle and, with the stick in his hand,
again went on his way. As he walked he thought
with pleasure of how he would be able to exercise
the stick on his brothers, and how pleased his father
would be to always have water for the king's flocks,
even though he should be in the midst of dry fields
and woods. Then he thought of his mother's surprise
at finding he had got the wonderful cloth. All of
a sudden he met a soldier clothed in rags, lame,

and covered with scars. He had once been a fine warrior, and, addressing the young man, he said—

"Evil luck follows me, a man who has been a good soldier, and who has fought well in his youth. What has been the good of it all? I am lamed for life, and upon this lonely road I cannot even get anything to eat. Take pity on me, and give me at least a piece of bread."

The fool sat down, spread his cloth, and said—

"Wonderful cloth, let him who is hungry and thirsty find here everything he wants."

Immediately they heard a hissing noise in the air, something shone above them, and they found a fine table, spread as for a royal feast in front of them. They ate and drank, and then the table disappeared. As the simpleton was about to continue his journey, the soldier said—

"Will you give me your cloth in exchange for this hat with six corners. It shoots of itself, and hits, in an instant, whatever you wish. You have only to turn it round on your head, and say—'Hat which fires, to please me, strike what I tell you.' Then it shoots with such a sure aim that if your enemy were a mile away he would bite the dust."

The lad thought it would be well to have the hat, for how useful would it be in time of danger, and when he wished to serve his king and country. So he gave the cloth to the soldier, tied the girdle

again round his waist, put the hat upon his head,
took his stick in his hand, and went on once more.

He had not gone far when he thought of what
the oak had told him about the cloth, and of how
he wanted to surprise his mother with it. So he
said to his stick—

"Stick, that beats of itself, go quickly and look
for my cloth. Go, I want it back."

The cudgel went off after the soldier, overtook
him, and commenced to beat him, crying—

"So you seek the wealth of others, do you?
Take that, knave, and that."

The soldier, who was lusty in spite of his wounds,
set himself on his guard, and would have given blow
for blow, but the stick laid on so rapidly that he
at last gave in. Overcome by the pain, he threw
down the cloth and fled. The stick took the cloth
to its master, who continued his journey.

At length he came out of the wood. He crossed
over the fields, and already saw his father's house
before him, when he met his brothers, who, running
to him, said impatiently—

"Well, simpleton, where are the golden acorns?"

The lad looked at them, laughed, and said to his
stick—

"Stick, which beats of itself, punish those who
have offended me."

The stick at once left the hands of the lad and
commenced to lay itself on the brothers, crying—

"You have done your brother enough wrong. Now, then, suffer yourselves in your turn."

The brothers were as much astounded as if a kettle of hot water had fallen about their ears. They cried out and ran off, disappearing in a cloud of dust. The stick at length came back to its master, who entered the house, climbed up on the stove, and, calling his mother, told her all that had happened. Then he said—

"Wonderful cloth, let him who is hungry and thirsty find here all he wants."

A whistling was heard, something came sparkling in the air, and they found before them a table spread as if for a king's banquet. There were dishes, glasses, and goblets of hydromel and wine, and all the things were of gold or silver. The simpleton and his mother for a time admired the feast, and then, just as they were sitting down to it, the door opened and his father came in. He was thunderstruck when he saw the table, but, being invited to share the good things with them, quickly sat down and fell to. When they had finished the whistling noise was again heard, and all the things disappeared.

The shepherd went off to the Court to tell the king all about these wonderful things, and the king despatched an officer to the fool. When he came into the house he found the simpleton lying on the stove, and said to him—

"If you love your life, listen and obey the orders of the king. You are to send him by myself the wonderful cloth which provides feasts of itself, and for this you shall be honoured by the royal favour. If you do not comply, you shall remain in your present wretched condition, and shall, moreover, receive the punishment of a disobedient fellow. Do you understand me?"

"Oh yes," said the lad, "I understand you;" and then he quietly said—

"Stick, which beats of itself, give those who deserve them some good blows."

With the speed of lightning the stick left the fool's hands. Three times it alighted on the officer's body, and then he fled. The stick, however, was not content to let him off so easily, and it followed him, beating him all the time, and crying—

"Promises befool children. Don't make them too rashly. To teach you better, take that, knave, and that."

Beaten and bewildered, the officer returned to the king and told him all, and when his majesty heard that the lad had a stick which beat of its own accord, he longed so much for it that he quite forgot the cloth. So he sent off some of his soldiers to the lad with orders to bring the stick. The soldiers came to the hut and found the fool on the stove.

"Give us the cudgel," said they. "The king

will give you what you ask for it. If you will not give it to us we shall take it."

Instead of making a reply, the lad put on his girdle, and said—

"Wonderful girdle, for my safety, and not for my pleasure, let me find myself on the water."

There was a murmuring in the air, and a great change took place. A magnificent lake—long, wide, and deep—appeared in the middle of the plain, and in it swam fish with golden scales and eyes of pearls. In the middle of the lake, in a silver skiff, was a man whom the soldiers recognised as the fool. For a time they looked on in wonder, and then they set off to tell the king all about it. When the king heard of such a girdle he longed to have it. He took counsel with his officer, and then sent off a whole battalion of soldiers to take the fool prisoner.

This time they tried to catch him while he was asleep. Just as they were about to lay hands on him, however, the fool turned his hat, and said—

"Hat that shoots, to please me, strike those who trouble me."

At that instant a hundred bullets whistled in the air. The place rang with the noise of guns, and the air was filled with smoke. Some of the soldiers fell dead on the ground, others ran off to hide them- selves in the woods, and some went to tell the king.

The king was dreadfully angry to think that he could not get the better of the fool. He had desired to have the cloth, to have the stick, to have the girdle, but what were any of these things to the wonderful six-cornered hat which, of its own accord, fired and shot down its opponents as well as if it had been a battery of cannon !

Having considered for some time, he thought it would, perhaps, be best to try persuasion. So he sent to the lad's mother, and said to her—

"Tell your son, the fool, that I and my lovely daughter salute him, and we beg of him to come to the palace and show us all the wonderful things we are told he possesses. If he is willing to make me a present of them I will give him half my kingdom, and will name him as my successor in the throne. My daughter also will take him for her husband."

The mother ran off to her son, and persuaded him to accept the king's invitation, and go to the palace with his wonderful treasures. The lad fastened on his girdle, put on his hat, hid the cloth in his bosom, took his stick in his hand, and set off to the Court. When he came there the king was engaged, but the lad was received very politely by his attendants. Music struck up as he came to the palace, the soldiers presented arms, and altogether the lad was received very much better than he could have expected. At length, when he was introduced into the hall in which was the king, the lad took off his hat and bowed.

"What," said he, "O king, do you desire? I have come to lay at the foot of your throne the cloth, the girdle, the stick, and the hat. In return for these presents I only ask that your royal favour may light on the humblest of your subjects."

"Tell me then, fool," said the king, "how much money do you want for those things?"

"Money," replied the lad, "a fool like me does not want money. The king promised my mother to give me half his kingdom, and his daughter in marriage. I only ask so much!"

The king's officer signed to the soldiers to come in. They laid hands on the lad suddenly, dragged him out into the courtyard, and there, while the drums beat and the trumpets sounded, they killed him and buried him.

As the soldiers pierced him to the heart, some drops of blood sprang forth, and fell under the windows of the princess, who wept at the sight and shed tears on the reddened earth. Wonderful to tell! from these drops of blood there sprang up an apple-tree which grew till it reached the windows of the princess's apartments. When the princess laid her hand on the boughs of the tree, an apple fell off into her bosom. The princess took it up and played with it.

The next day, when night came on, all were

122 RUSSIAN AND POLISH FOLKLORE.

asleep in the palace save the guards, the king's officer, and the princess. The guards were watching, as usual, with their arms in their hands. The princess was playing with the apple, and could not sleep. As for the king's officer, soon after he lay down he was roused by a terrible noise. The cudgel appeared before him, and though he ran round and round his chamber, it pursued and beat him, crying—

"You good-for-nothing fellow! Don't be so envious and unjust. Don't return evil for good, and steal what belongs to others. Take that, and that, and that!"

The officer called aloud and cried for mercy, but the stick still laid on.

The princess, hearing some one groaning, began to weep, and then a wonderful thing happened. Some of her tears fell on the apple. It grew, changed its form, and, all of a sudden, there stood before her a fine young man, the very same as had been slain under her window.

"Fair princess," said he, "I salute you. The treachery of the king's officer caused my death, and your tears have recalled me to life again. Your father promised to give you to me for my wife: what do you say?"

"If it is my father's wish," replied the princess, "I consent," and she gave him her hand.

The lad spoke some words and the doors opened

of themselves. The six-cornered hat came and placed itself on his head, the girdle came and wound itself around his waist, the cloth hid itself in one of his pockets, and the avenging cudgel placed itself in his hands.

When this had taken place the king came running in. How astonished was he to see the fool alive,. and there! The lad did not await for the king to give vent to his rage, but said—

"Wonderful girdle, for my safety, and not for my pleasure, let me find myself on the water."

There was a murmuring in the air. A wonderful change took place. A large, wide, and deep lake appeared in the middle of the palace grounds. In the crystal waters played fish with golden scales and eyes of pearl. Afar off on the water were the fool and the princess. The king came to the side of the lake and beckoned the lad to him. He came, and with the princess knelt at the king's feet, and told him how they two were in love with one another. The king gave them his blessing. The lake disappeared, and the three returned to the palace, when the king, calling his counsellors, told them all that had occurred. Then he named the fool as his successor on the throne, gave him his daughter, and threw his officer into prison.

In return, the lad gave the king the cloth, the stick, the girdle, and the hat, telling him how to use them, and teaching him the magic words. The next day the marriage took place, and, with his daughter, the king gave the lad half of his dominions, and in the evening there was a royal feast, so grand that the like was never before seen or heard of.

THE EVIL EYE.

I.

THERE was once upon a time a rich gentleman who lived in a fine house on the banks of the Vistula. All the windows in the house looked towards the river, none looked towards the wide sweep of country around. The path under the poplars which led up to the house was overgrown with grass and weeds, and showed plainly enough that none of the neighbours visited there, and that very little of the old hospitality was to be experienced there.

The gentleman who owned the house had lived there for seven years, and had come from some far-off place. The peasants knew little about him, and they avoided him with fear and trembling, for there were terrible tales about him.

The gentleman was born on the banks of the river Sau, and his parents had been rich. Misfortune, however, had pursued him from the cradle upwards. He had an evil eye, which scattered disease and death wherever its glances fell. If he by ill chance glanced over his herd, the cattle on which

his eye fell died.   Whatever he loved would surely
die.   His own parents, to complete the son's sorrow,
perished, and the man with the evil eye, as he came
to be called in his birthplace, where the evil eye
had caused so much mischief, sold everything he
had, and set off to the banks of the Vistula, where
he bought the fine house.   He kept no folk about
him save one old manservant, who had nursed him
in his arms when he was a boy, and on whom the
evil eye of his master had no effect.

The unlucky man seldom went out of his house,
for he knew that his glance brought misfortune,
disease, and death on what it lighted on.   When he
did go out in his carriage his old servant sat beside
him, and told him when they were coming to a
man, a village, or a town.   Then the miserable
man would either cover his eyes with his hands, or
cast down his glances on the floor of his carriage,
where he always had a bundle of pea-stalks at his
feet.[1]

So it was that he had all the windows of his fine
house made to look over the Vistula.   Twice had
he by ill chance looked upon his farm-buildings,
and they had been set on fire by his glance.

In spite of all his care the sailors cursed him,
and pointed with fear to the wide windows of his
beautiful house, out of which he scattered destruc-

[1] When the evil eye is directed to a bundle of pea-stalks
it does no damage, but merely dries up the stalks.

tion amongst them, the stream rushing on fast in the channel, and bringing many a ship to ground opposite the White House, as the place was called.

One boatman determined to see the man. He jumped into his boat and set off to the house. When he arrived there he asked to see the master. The old servant, fearful of the consequences, led him into the room. His master was dining, and being put out that he should be interrupted at his meal, he frowned upon the stranger. Immediately a fever took the sailor, and he sank down on the floor at the door.

The old servant, at the command of his master, took the man to his boat, gave him some money, and rowed him back to the other side of the river. The poor sailor was ill for a long time, and when he regained his strength he gave such a terrible account of the White House, and of its master, as greatly increased the fear of his comrades. From that time, when they went down the river in their boats and came opposite to the White House, they would turn their eyes away, and pray heartily that they might be protected from the evil glance of the terrible man who lived there.

II.

Three years had passed, and the White House was still the dread of the neighbours and the terror of the sailors. No one came to see the much-feared man, and he lived solitary and miserable.

The next winter was very severe. The wolves, coming together, howled with hunger around the house, and the master sat by the hearth, on which burned a large fire, and sorrowfully turned over the leaves of a large book. The old servant had secured all the doors, and sat at the other side of the room warming himself, and busied in mending a fishing-net.

"Stanislas," said his master, "have you caught any fish?"

"Not many, master, but as many as we two shall want."

"That is true," said his master. "Although so many years have passed, we are but two. O unlucky hour in which I was born! Here am I alone, and all men fly from me as if I were a monster," and the tears fell in a torrent from his unfortunate eyes.

All of a sudden they heard a voice crying for help. The master started. It was a long time since he had heard a strange voice. The old servant rushed out, and his master followed him with the light in his hand.

Before the door stood a covered sledge, and by it was an old man who called for help.

As soon as the stranger saw the two men coming to him, he lifted his wife, who had fainted, out of the sledge, and the old servant helped the terrified daughter, a beautiful girl, to alight.

They put on more wood, and brought the fainted lady round, and the master of the house, pleased to be able to show hospitality, went and fetched some old wine in order to drink the strangers' healths. The old servant laughed to himself as he marked his master's joyful face. The strange guest, cheered by the wine, told how they had lost their way, how they had fallen in with a pack of hungry wolves, and how their fleet horse had carried them to the White House.

Towards night the luggage was taken out of the sledge, and the wearied travellers retired to rest in warm, comfortable chambers. All was still in the White House, save that the fire now and then sent forth a glimmering flame.

III.

It was within an hour of midnight, and the old servant was asleep by the fireside, when the door of his master's bedchamber opened and the unhappy man trod lightly into the hall. The old servant, wondering whether he was dreaming, rubbed his eyes, and said—

"What, cannot my master sleep?"

"Be quiet, old friend!" said his master in a joyful voice. "I cannot sleep, and do not wish to sleep when I am so happy as I now am."

And he sat down in a big arm-chair by the fire-side, smiled, and commenced to weep.

"Weep, poor master, weep," said Stanislas to himself. "Maybe you may weep your evil eyes away."

"Would that God would give me what I now wish," said his master, "and I would ask for nothing more in the world. Here have I lived thirty years like a hermit or a criminal, and yet I have never willingly hurt any one, and my soul is free from sin, but my eyes, my eyes!"

His countenance, which was so happy till now, became gloomy as usual; but soon a smile appeared on his face, as hope once more chased away sorrow.

"Dear friend!" said he, and Stanislas looked at him, "maybe I shall marry."

"Heaven help us!" cried the old servant. "But where then is your future bride?"

The master rose from his chair, walked on tiptoe to the side-door, which led to the chambers where slept the travellers, and, pointing to the door, said—

"There."

Stanislas nodded his head, as if he approved of his master's choice, and cheerfully put some wood upon the fire. His master went back to his room in deep thought, and the old servant mumbled to himself—

"Heaven grant it! But pears don't grow on willow-trees."

And he was soon asleep.

IV.

On the following morning the traveller rose rested and refreshed, but he was not able to continue his journey in consequence of the illness of his wife.

The master of the house was pleased when he heard that the strangers must pass some more days in his house, and old Stanislas began almost to think that the pears might grow on the willows after all.

The stranger was not exactly a rich man, but he had enough, was deemed an honest man, and lived honourably. He was much pleased with his friendly host, and as he was one day talking to his wife, who had much improved in her health, he said—

"Margaret, it strikes me that our host is in love with our daughter Mary, and, from what I can see, I think she does not dislike him. I cannot but be pleased with it."

"Oh," said his wife, "you only imagine it." But she was secretly pleased that her husband had no objection to what she had herself very much wished.

"The man is not poor, he has lived here a long time, he has proved himself a gentleman," went on the husband, walking up and down the room, "and our daughter is old enough to be married and take on her the cares of a household."

In the evening the husband, having partaken of the host's good wine, stroked his grey moustache with satisfaction, and listened with joy when the master of the house asked for his daughter's hand.

"My brother," said he after a short pause, " I am pleased with you, and since you ask no dowry with my daughter, and you have enough to live upon, she shall be your wife."

Three months later the terrible man took his wife home. The grass and weeds were cleared from the avenue of poplars, and many horses and carriages passed along it to and fro, as relations and friends of the beautiful bride came in troops to the wedding at the White House. In a few days, however, all was still again, and fresh grass and weeds began to grow in the avenue under the poplars.

V.

The winter was at hand, and the inmates of the White House only numbered one more—the mistress of the house.

Most of the servants whom the master had engaged ran away at once as soon as they heard he had an evil eye, and those who stayed a while, having been taken ill, soon left the house also.

The young, beautiful wife lay ill upon her rich bed.

Near her was her husband, who, with averted eyes, pressed her cold hand.

The poor wife knew well how terrible was her husband's glance. She knew that through it her suffering and sorrow were increased ; but still, in her love for the sorrowing man, she asked him to look upon her once more.

"My Mary," said the wretched man, with a deep sigh. "I shall never be happy with you so long as I have my eyes. Cut them out, then. Here is a sharp knife, and at your hand it will cause me no pain."

The poor wife shuddered at this terrible proposal, and the wretched man sank from his chair to the floor, and commenced to weep bitterly.

"Of what use is this gift of Heaven to me ?" cried he. "Of what use is it to me to possess the pleasures men have in sight, when my eyes scatter destruction and ruin around ? You are ill, my Mary. Why, a tree itself would wither when I cast my glance upon it in an evil hour. Take courage, though. Upon our child these eyes shall never look. Him they shall never harm, and he shall not have reason to curse his father."

A groan was the only answer of the sick wife.

The master called in a servant and left the room. All at once two different cries were heard from the two opposite sides of the White House.

From one side came the cry of a new-born child,

from the other side, in the hall where the fire
burned, came the cry of a man in pain. The one
was the cry of an infant as it looked upon the light
for the first time, the other was the cry of a man
who had bid farewell to sight for ever.

VI.

Six years later there were windows in the White
House from which one could obtain a fine view of the
village and the surrounding country. The sailors
had begun to make the House a resting-place on
their way down the stream. The mistress was well
and merry, and her great joy was a beautiful little
daughter who led her blind father about.

The country-folk, who had fled in terror from
the miserable man, now came up to him in friendship, when they saw him blind and taking a walk
led by his little daughter. The former stillness
departed. The servants filled the once empty halls
of the White House.

Old Stanislas had on that terrible day buried his
master's eyes in the garden. One day he wondered
what had become of them, and whether he could
find them. So he dug for them. All of a sudden
the eyes glared on him with a bright light. Hardly
had the glance fallen on his face when he stumbled
and, falling to the ground, died.

That was the first time the evil eyes had done
him hurt, and it was the last time their power was

exerted. They had done him no hurt while his master kept them, because, as he loved his servant, his heart had destroyed their power. Now they were in the earth they had acquired power for fresh evil, and killed the honest old man!

His blind master sorrowed long for him, and over his grave he placed a fine cross, near which the sailors often offered up a prayer when they landed at the White House.

THE SEVEN BROTHERS.

ONCE upon a time there lived an old man and an old woman, who had been married many years and had no children, and when they were yet old they prayed to God to give them a child who might help them in their work as they advanced in years. Their prayer was heard. When seven years had passed the old woman gave birth to seven sons, and they were all called Simeon. When the children were ten years old the old man and his wife died, and the sons began to till his ground.

It chanced that one day the Czar Ados came past, and, seeing them working in the fields, he was astonished to see such little fellows doing such work. He sent one of his nobles to ask whose children they were. So the noble came to them and asked who they were who worked so hard. The eldest Simeon told him that they were orphans and had no one to work for them. As for their names they were all called Simeon.

When the Czar got back to the palace he called together all his nobles and asked them their opinion, saying—

"My lords, there are seven orphans who have no kinsfolk. I will make them such men that they shall be grateful to me. Now, I want your advice as to what trade or art I shall have them taught."

Then all answered—

"Gracious sire, since they are old enough and have ability, we think it would be best to ask each of them what trade or art he wishes to learn."

The Czar was pleased with this advice, and asked the eldest Simeon—

"Tell me, friend, what trade or art would you like to learn? I will see that you are instructed in it."

The lad answered—

"May it please your majesty, I wish to learn no art, but if you will order a smithy to be built in the middle of your court, I will smithy a column which shall reach to heaven."

The Czar saw that this Simeon required no teaching, since he was such a smith, for he showed him very costly work, but he did not believe that he would be able to smithy a column that should reach to heaven. However, he ordered a place to be built in the middle of his yard, and the eldest Simeon set to work.

Then the Czar asked the second Simeon—

"And you, my friend, what art will you learn?"

"Your majesty," said he, "I do not wish to learn any business or trade, but when my brother has finished the column, I will stand on the top of it, look around into all the countries, and let you know what is passing in each of them."

The Czar perceived that there was no need to teach this lad anything, since he was so clever already.

Then he said to the third Simeon—

"What business or what art will you learn?"

"Your majesty," said he, "I do not wish to learn either handiwork or art, but if my eldest brother will make me an axe, I will build a ship in an instant."

"Such a man do I want," said the Czar. "You, too, have nothing to learn."

"And you," said the Czar to the fourth Simeon, "what handiwork or what art do you wish to learn?"

"Your majesty," said he, "I do not wish to learn anything, but, when my brother has finished his ship, and it is attacked by the enemy, I will seize it by the prow, carry it to the underground kingdom, and, when the enemy is gone, I will put it again on the sea."

The Czar was very much astonished, and said—

"You, too, have nothing to learn."

Then he spoke to the fifth brother—

"And you, Simeon, what handiwork or what art will you learn?"

"I want to learn nothing, your majesty," said he, "but if my eldest brother will make me a gun, I

.will shoot with it any bird that flies, however far off it be, so that I am able to see it."

"You will be an excellent sportsman," said the Czar.

Then he asked the sixth brother—

"Well, Simeon, what art do you wish to learn?"

"I wish to learn no art, your majesty," said he, "but if my fifth brother shoots a bird, I will catch it before it comes to the ground and bring it to your majesty."

"That is very clever," said the Czar. "You will do instead of a dog in the field."

Then the Czar asked the last brother—

"And you, Simeon, what handiwork or art will you learn?"

"I want to learn neither handiwork nor art, your majesty," replied he, "for I already know a precious art."

"What is it," asked the Czar, "that is so good?"

"I am so skilful at stealing," said he, "that no one can beat me at it."

When the Czar heard that the lad was acquainted with such a wicked art, he was angry, and said to his nobles—

"My lords, let me have your advice as to how this thief, Simeon, should be punished. What death should he die?"

"Your majesty," said they all, "why should he

die? It is, not unlikely, since he is such a clever thief, that he may prove useful in some case."

"How so?" asked the Czar.

"Your majesty," said they, "has during the last ten years sought the hand of the Czarina, the beautiful Helena, in vain, and lost many armies and much treasure. Now this thief, Simeon, may devise some means of stealing the Czarina for your Majesty."

"You say well, my friends," observed the Czar, and he went and said to the thief—

"Now, Simeon, can you wander over seven and twenty countries into the thirtieth and steal for me the beautiful princess, Helena? I love her very much, and if you procure her for me you shall be well rewarded."

"We will see to it," said he, "you have but to command."

"I do not merely command," said the Czar, "but I beg of you not to remain longer at my court, but to take what armies you wish to effect your purpose."

"I do not want either your armies or your treasure," said the thief. "Only send all of us together, for I can do nothing without the others."

The Czar did not wish for all the brothers to go, but though he thought it hard, he was obliged to consent.

In the meantime the eldest brother had completed the iron column in the smithy in the court of the palace. The second brother climbed up to the top, and from there he saw the kingdom of the fair Helena's father. He called out to the Czar Ados—

"Your majesty, beyond twenty-seven countries in the thirtieth there sits, at a window, the Czarina, the beautiful Helena. How fair she is! One can see every blue vein in her white skin."

Then the Czar was more in love with her than ever, and cried out to the Simeons—

"My friends, set out as quickly as you can and return soon. I can live no longer without the beautiful Helena."

The eldest Simeon smithied a gun for the third brother, and carried bread for the journey. The thief took with him a cat, and so they set out. Now the thief had so trained the cat that it ran after him everywhere, just like a dog, and when he stood still it stood by him, on its hind-legs, rubbing against him and purring. So they went on till they came to the shore of a sea over which they must pass. For a long time they walked about on the shore and looked for wood, in order to build a ship, and at last they came to a great oak. The third brother took his axe and cut away at the root. The oak was brought to the ground, and a ship was in a moment built from it, filled with all kinds of precious things. The brothers entered the ship and sailed away.

After some months they came to the place they

sought, and cast anchor in the harbour. The next day the thief, taking his cat, went into the town, and, coming to the Czar's palace, stood in front of the Princess Helena's window. His cat at once stood up on its hind-legs and began to rub itself against him, and to purr. Now a cat had never before been seen in that kingdom, nor, indeed, had the people knowledge that there was any such animal.

The princess sat at the window, and, when she saw the cat, she sent out her servants and maids to ask Simeon if he would sell it, and if so, what he wanted for it. The servants came to Simeon, and asked him what kind of animal the cat was, and whether he would sell it.

" Tell her majesty, the beautiful Helena," said the thief, " that the animal is called a cat. I cannot sell it, but, if her majesty pleases, I desire the honour of making her a present of it."

The attendants took the message to the princess, who, when she heard it, was delighted, and coming out of her chamber she asked Simeon why he would not sell the cat.

" I cannot sell the cat, your majesty," said he, " but, if you please, I will give it to you."

The princess took the cat in her arms, and going back to her apartment, told Simeon to follow. When they were in the palace, she went to her father, the Czar Say, showed him the cat, and told him that a stranger had given it to her. The Czar was very much pleased with the strange animal, and ordered that the thief Simeon should be brought to him. When he came, the Czar wished to give him treasures in return for the cat, but, as Simeon refused all, the Czar said to him : " My friend, stay for a while in my palace. The cat will become more familiar to my daughter if you are here."

Simeon, however, did not wish to stay, and said—

" It would give me the greatest pleasure, your majesty, to stay in your palace if I had not a ship in which I came to your country, and which I can leave in charge of no one. If, however, your majesty wishes it, I will come every day to the palace, and get the cat accustomed to your daughter."

So the Czar ordered him to come. Simeon went every day to the beautiful Princess Helena, and one day he said to her—

" Gracious lady, I have come a long while to you, but I have noticed that you never go out. Would you not like to see my vessel? I could show you fine goods, gold-stuff, and diamonds, such as you have never seen."

The princess went away to her father, and begged his permission for her to take a walk on the quay. The Czar gave it her, but told her to take her attendants and maids with her. So the princess went with Simeon. When they had come to the quay, Simeon invited the princess on board his vessel, and, calling his brothers to show her all the various goods, he said, after a time—

"Tell your servants and maids to leave the ship so that I can show you some costly things they must not see."

So the princess bade them leave the vessel. When she was alone, the thief ordered his brothers to cut the cable, set all sail, and put out to sea. In the meanwhile he amused the princess, showing her the things, and giving presents to her. So they spent several hours examining the goods. At last the princess told him that it was time for her to go home, as the Czar would be expecting her. But when she went up out of the cabin, she saw that the vessel was already far out at sea, and that she was far away from the coast. Then she beat upon her breast, changed herself to a swan, and flew upwards; but the fifth Simeon, seizing his gun, shot at her, and the sixth caught her as she was falling into the water and brought her to the vessel. The princess became a young woman once more.

The attendants and maids, who had gone to the quay with the princess, and had seen the ship sail away with her, told the Czar of the trick Simeon had played them, and he ordered that all his fleet should go in pursuit. It had come near to Simeon's vessel, when the fourth brother laid hold of the vessel by the prow and dragged it off to the underground kingdom. The sailors of the fleet saw the vessel vanish, and they thought that it had sunk with the beautiful princess ; so, going back to the Czar Say, they told him of the ship's disappearance.

The brothers came safely home, and led the fair Princess Helena to the Czar Ados, who gave the Simeons, in reward for their great service, their freedom and much gold, silver, and many precious stones. And he lived with the princess for many years, prosperous and happy.

SILA CZAROVITCH AND IVASCHKA.

THERE was once upon a time a Czar called Chotei, who had three sons. The first was called Aspe, the second Adam, and the third, the youngest, Sila. The elder brothers came to their father and asked him to let them go and travel in other countries, so that they might see the world and learn how things were. The Czar gave them his permission, and let them each have a vessel in which they might sail. Then the youngest brother came to the Czar and asked him to let him go with his brothers.

"My dear son," said the Czar, "you. are too young to bear the fatigues of a journey. Stop here then at home, and do not think of going abroad."

Sila, however, wished very much to see the strange countries, and so wearied his father with his prayers, that at last he gave him his permission to go, and let him have a vessel also. As soon as the three brothers were on board their ships they set sail. When they came to the open sea, however, the eldest brother's vessel went on first, the second brother's next, and Sila's came last.

As they sailed, the third day there came floating

past them a coffin with iron bands. The two eldest brothers saw it, but did not pick it up. When Sila, however, saw it, he gave orders to his sailors to secure it, bring it on board, and bury it when they came to a suitable spot. On the following day a great storm came on, and Sila's ship, being driven out of its proper course, drifted to the steep shores of an unknown land. When they arrived there, Sila ordered the sailors to carry the coffin on shore, and he followed it himself and saw it buried in the earth.

Sila then told the ship's master to stop where the vessel was for three years, waiting for him. If he did not come back at the end of that time, he told the man he was to sail away. Then Sila took leave of his captain and his men, and went away following his eyes. For a long time he went on and met no one. On the third day, however, he heard a man running after him, clothed in white. When he saw that the man was coming up to him, he drew his sword, fearing that the stranger might intend to do him some hurt. But when the man came up to him, he fell down at his feet, and began to thank him for having rescued him. Sila, not understanding what he meant, asked him why he thanked him, and what good service he had done him. The unknown sprang to his feet, and said—

"Sila Czarovitch, how can I ever repay you? There I lay in my coffin, which you took on board and buried on the land, and so was I rescued from the sea."

"How came you in the coffin?" asked Sila.

"I will tell you all," said the man. "I was once a great magician, and my mother, fearing that I did a great deal of harm to folk by my magic, confined me in the coffin, and turned me out upon the sea. I have been floating for over a hundred years, and no one ever picked me up. You I have to thank for my deliverance, and in return for it I will aid you in any way I can. Tell me, do you not wish to marry? If you do, I know the beautiful Queen Truda, who would make you a worthy wife."

Sila told him that if the queen were beautiful he would be content to marry her. Ivaschka, in the white grave-clothes, assured him that she was the most beautiful woman in all the world, and Sila, when he heard that, asked his companion to go with him to her country. So they went on together.

Now Queen Truda's kingdom was surrounded by a fence with posts, and on every post, save one, was a man's head. When Sila saw that he was alarmed, and asked Ivaschka what it meant.

"Those," said Ivaschka, "are the heads of the warriors who came to ask the Queen Truda to marry them."

Sila was afraid when he heard that, and wished himself back again in his own kingdom. He did not wish to go on and see the father of the queen, but Ivaschka told him he had nothing to fear if he went on boldly with him. So Sila and he went on together.

When they had entered the kingdom, Ivaschka said to him—

"Listen, Sila Czarovitch, I will live with you as your servant. When you come to the royal apartments, behave humbly to King Salom. He will ask you where you come from, what country you belong to, who your father is, what is your name, and on what errand you have come. Tell him all, and do not try to conceal anything. Tell him that you have come to ask for his daughter's hand, and he will give her to you with the greatest joy."

Sila went into the palace, and when King Salom saw him he came to meet him, took him by the white hands, led him into the white marble room, and said to him—

"Young man, who are you? From what kingdom do you come? Who is your father? What is your name? and why are you come?"

"I have come," replied Sila, "from the kingdom of the Czar Chotei; I am known as Sila Czarovitch, and I have come here to ask for your daughter, the beautiful Queen Truda, for my wife."

Then King Salom was very pleased when he heard that the son of so famous a Czar desired to wed his daughter, and he at once sent to her, to tell her to get ready for the wedding. When

the day came, the king commanded all the princes
and nobles to come to the palace. From there they
went to the church, and Sila Czarovitch married the
beautiful Queen Truda. The company went back
to the palace, seated themselves at table, and ate
and drank with great joy.

When evening was come Ivaschka came near to
Sila, and said to him softly—

"Listen, Sila Czarovitch. When you retire with
your wife, take care you do not say a word to her, or
you are a dead man, and your head will find a place
on the last post. She will do all she can to make
you speak, but do not you say a word to her."

Sila asked him why he gave him this warning.

"She is," said Ivaschka, "acquainted with a
spirit which flies through the air in the shape of a
dragon with six heads. Your wife will lay her
hand upon your breast. When she does so,
spring up and beat her with a stick till she has no
strength left in her. I will myself watch at the
door of the room."

The queen did, as Ivaschka foretold, do all
she could to make Sila speak, but he would not
utter a word. Then Truda put her hand on his
breast, and pressed him, so that he could hardly
breathe. Sila jumped up, seized a stick, which
Ivaschka had put there for the occasion, and commenced to beat her as if he would kill her. Immediately there came on a terrible storm, and there

flew into the room a six-headed dragon who commenced to attack Sila. Then Ivaschka came in with a sharp sword in his hand, and he and the dragon fought together for three hours, when Ivaschka managed to cut off two of the dragon's heads, and the monster flew away. Ivaschka then told Sila he might go to sleep and fear nothing. So Sila laid him down and slept till morning.

King Salom was anxious respecting his son-in-law, and he sent early in the morning to ask if all was well with him. When he heard that it was, he was delighted, for he remembered the fate of the others who had come to marry his daughter. He summoned Sila to him, and they spent the whole day in merriment.

The next night Ivaschka warned Sila that he must not speak to his wife, and he himself took up his station outside the door of the room. Sila's wife again tried to make him speak, and again put her hand upon his breast, and Sila leaped up and thrashed her. The dragon flew in and attacked him, but Ivaschka sprang in from the door with the sword in his hand, and after he and the dragon had fought for three hours Ivaschka cut off two more of its heads. Then the dragon flew off and Sila lay down to sleep. The king again sent for Sila to come to him, and they spent the day together very pleasantly.

The third night Ivaschka warned Sila as before,

and Sila did as he was bid. Ivaschka again fought with the monster, and, cutting off the two last heads, he burnt them and the carcass, and scattered the ashes over the fields.

So Sila Czarovitch stayed with his father-in-law for a whole year, and then Ivaschka, coming to him one day, told him to ask the king to give him permission to return home. Sila went to King Salom and obtained his leave to go, and the king sent two divisions of his army with him as an escort. So Sila parted with his father-in-law, and set off with his wife for his own land.

When they were half-way home Ivaschka told Sila to stop and camp there. Sila did as he advised, and ordered his tent to be put up. On the next day Ivaschka took some pieces of stick and burnt them in front of the Czarovitch's tent. Then he came to the tent, led Queen Truda outside, and unsheathing his sword he cut her in two. Sila was greatly terrified, and commenced to weep when he saw that.

"Do not weep," said Ivaschka, "she will come to life again."

As soon as the Queen was cut in two there came out of her all manner of evil spirits, and all of these Ivaschka threw into the fire. Then said he to Sila—

"Do you see the evil things which possessed your wife? They are all evil spirits which had entered her."

.When all the evil spirits were destroyed in the fire, he placed the two parts of Truda's body together, sprinkled them with water from a running brook, and the queen became alive again. She was now also as good as she had before been evil.

Then said Ivaschka to Sila—

"Good-bye, Sila Czarovitch, you will see me no more;" and as soon as he had spoken those words he disappeared.

Sila struck his tent and went on homewards, and when he came to the spot where he had left his ship, he dismissed the troops that accompanied him, went on board with his queen, and set sail. He soon came to his own land, and his arrival there was greeted with the sound of cannon. Czar Chotei came to meet him, and taking him and his wife by their white hands he led them into the white marble room. Then there was a feast prepared, and they ate and drank and were merry. Sila lived with his father two years, and then he went back to the country of his father-in-law, King Salom. He succeeded him on the throne, and reigned with his beautiful Queen Truda, during many years, with much love and happiness.

THE STOLEN HEART.

ONCE upon a time there stood, on an island in the Vistula, a great castle surrounded by a strong rampart. At each corner was a tower, and from these there waved in the wind many a flag, while the soldiers stood on guard upon them. A bridge connected the island with the banks of the river.

In this castle lived a knight, a brave and famous warrior. When the trumpets sounded from the battlements of the castle, their notes announced that he had returned from victory loaded with booty.

In the deep dungeons of the castle many a prisoner was confined, and they were led out daily to work. They had to keep the ramparts in repair, and to see to the garden. Now among these prisoners was an old woman, who was a sorceress. She swore that she would be revenged upon the knight for his ill-treatment of her, and patiently awaited an opportunity to effect her purpose.

One day the knight came back wearied out with his exertions on one of his warlike excursions. He

154

lay down upon the grass, closed his eyes, and was soon fast asleep.

The witch seized the opportunity. Coming gently to him, she scattered poppy seed on his eyes so that he should sleep the sounder. Then, with an aspen branch, she struck him on the breast over his heart.

The knight's breast at once opened, so that one could look in and see the heart as it lay there and beat. The sorceress laughed, stretched out her bony arm, and with her long fingers she stole away the heart so quietly that the knight never woke.

Then the woman took a hare's heart which she had ready, put it in the sleeping man's breast, and closed up the opening. Going away softly, she hid herself in a thicket, to see the effect of her wicked work.

Before the knight was even awake he began to feel the change that the hare's heart was making in him. He, who had till now never known fear, quaked and tossed himself uneasily from side to side. When he awoke he felt as if he should be crushed by his armour. The cry of his hounds, as it fell on his ear, filled him with terror.

Once he had loved to hear their deep baying as he followed them in pursuit of the prey in the wild forest, but now he was filled with fear, and fled like a timid hare. As he ran to his room the clang of his armour, the ringing of his silver spurs, the clatter of his spear, filled him with such terror that he threw all aside, and sank exhausted on his bed.

Even in his sleep fear pursued him. Once he dreamed only of battles, and of the prizes of victory, now he trembled as he dreamt. The barking of his dogs, the voices of his soldiers as they paced the ramparts while they watched, made him quake as he lay on his bed, and he buried his head, like a frightened child, in his pillow.

At length there came a body of the knight's enemies to besiege him in his castle. The knight's soldiers looked upon their leader, who had so often delighted in the excitement of the camp, and in the victory. In vain they waited for him to lead them forth. The once so brave knight, when he heard the clash of arms, the cry of the men, and the clang of the horses' hoofs, fled to the topmost chamber of his castle, and from there looked down upon the force which had come against him.

When he recollected his expeditions in the time past, his combats, his victories, he wept bitterly, and cried out aloud—

" O Heaven ! give me now courage, give me the old strength of heart and vigour. My men have already gone to the field, and I, who used to lead them, now, like a girl, look through the highest loop-hole upon my enemies. Give me my old boldness, that I may take my arms again; make me what I was once, and bless me with victory."

These thoughts, as it were, awakened him from a dream. He went again into his chamber, put on his armour, leaped upon his horse, and rode outside the castle gate. The soldiers saw him come with joy, and sounded the trumpets. The knight went on, but in his secret soul he was afraid, and when his men gallantly threw themselves upon the enemy, deadly fear came over him, and he turned and fled.

Even when he was once more in his stronghold, when the mighty walls held him safe within them, fear did not leave him. He sprang from his horse, fled to an innermost chamber, and there, quite unmanned, awaited inglorious death.

His men had triumphed over the foe, and the salutations of the guards announced their victorious return. All wondered at the flight of their leader at such a time. They looked for him, and discovered him half dead in a deep cellar.

The unfortunate knight did not live long. During the winter he tried to warm his quaking limbs by the fireside of his castle. When spring came he would open his window that he might breathe the fresh air, and one day it chanced a swallow, that had built its nest in a hole of the roof, struck him on the head with its wing. The blow was fatal. As if he had been struck by lightning, the knight fell down upon the ground, and in a short while died.

All his men mourned for their good master.

They knew not what had changed him, but about a year later, when some sorceresses were being put to the ordeal for having kept off the rain, one of them confessed that she had taken the knight's heart, and put in his breast a hare's heart in its place. Then the men knew how it was that a man who had formerly been so bold of heart had become so fearful. They mourned his misfortune, and, taking the witch to his grave, there they burnt her alive.

PRINCE SLUGOBYL.

THERE was once upon a time a king who had an only son named Slugobyl. The young prince was very fond of travelling, and when he was twenty years of age he begged his father and mother so much to let him go to see the world, that they gave him their consent, giving him as an attendant an old servant on whose fidelity they thought they could rely. The prince, well equipped and armed, mounted his horse, and, after having taken a tender leave, set off to distant countries in the hope of acquiring knowledge and returning wiser, and more fitted to rule.

As he rode along he saw a cygnet pursued by an eagle, which threatened to overtake it every moment. The prince seized his bow, and shot so well that the eagle, mortally wounded, fell at his feet. The cygnet seeing this stopped in its flight, and said to the prince—

" Prince Slugobyl, it is not a poor cygnet that thanks you, but the daughter of the Invisible Prince, who, changed into this shape, sought refuge from the pursuit of the giant Koshchei. My father will ·

159

reward you for this good action. Remember when
you have need of him, you have only to speak
these words thrice — 'Invisible Prince, come to
me.'"

When it had thus spoken, the cygnet flew away,
and the prince, having watched it till it was out of
sight, continued his journey. He went on for a
long time until he found himself in the midst of a
plain scorched up by the heat of the sun. Not a
tree, not a bush, not even a plant, was to be seen.
No bird flew by, no insect broke the stillness with
its hum. Everything seemed as if it had been
stricken with death by the sun's rays. The prince,
after having travelled some hours on this plain,
began to feel very thirsty, so he sent his servant
off to see if he could find some spring or well at
which he could alight. By good luck the servant
found a well, very deep, and containing plenty of
fresh water, but there was nothing by means of
which they could draw the water up. What should
they do? At length the prince said—

"Take the cord with which we secure our horses
and fasten it around you, and then I will let you
down into the well, for I am nearly dead with
thirst."

"My prince," answered the servant, "I am heavier
than you, and you are not so strong as I am. If I
go down you will never be able to draw me up again.
It would be better for you to go down the well,

and then I can pull you up when you have drunk as much as you wish."

The prince thought the advice good, and the servant tied the cord under his arms, and let him down into the well. When he had drunk as much as he wished, he got some of the water for his servant, and then he pulled the cord as a signal for him to draw him up. Instead of doing so, however, the servant looked down and said to him—

"Listen to me, prince. Since the day of your birth up to the present time you have had everything you wished for, while I have undergone great misery, and have slaved all my life. Now we will change places. Take your choice. Will you be my servant? If not, pray Heaven to have mercy on you, for I shall leave you to drown."

"Stop, my good servant," said the prince, "don't do that, I beg you. What good would it do you? You would never find so good a position as you have with me, and you know that murderers meet with a dreadful fate in the next world. Their hands are plunged in boiling pitch, their shoulders are scourged with red-hot iron, and their necks are sawn with wooden saws."

"I do not care for all that," said the servant, "but I know that I shall drown you unless you consent."

And he commenced to loosen the cord.

"Well then," said the prince, "I agree to what

Russian.   L you ask. You shall be my prince and I will be your servant. I pledge you my word."

"I don't believe in words," cried the servant, "which the wind blows away. Swear to me that you will confirm the promise in writing."

"I swear it," said the prince.

The servant let down a paper and pencil, and dictated the following words—

"I declare that I renounce my name and all my rights in favour of him who carries this paper, and that I take him for my prince, and will serve him.

Signed, in the well—

PRINCE SLUGOBYL."

The servant, who was unable to read, took the paper, drew the prince up out of the well, and then changed clothes with him. Thus disguised, the two went on for a week, until they entered a large town and came to the palace of the king. The false prince sent his companion to see to the horses, while he presented himself boldly to the king, and said to him—

"I am come, sire, to ask the hand of your beautiful and wise daughter, whose fame has spread even to my father's court. If you consent I assure you of our friendship, but if you refuse we shall make war with you."

"The request and the threat are alike unseasonable," said the king. "Listen, prince; I am willing to show my respect for the king, your father, by granting his request, on one condition. Our enemies, enraged against us, have assembled a large army, and now threaten our town. If you deliver us, my daughter is yours."

"Very well," replied the false prince, "I will utterly destroy the hostile army. Let them come as near as possible to the town. I promise you that I will acquit myself so well, that to-morrow morning you shall find no traces of them."

When it was evening, he called his pretended servant to him from his lodging in the stables, and, when the prince had respectfully saluted him, said—

"Listen, my friend. Go out at once and destroy the hostile army which is encamped outside the city, and do it so that folk will think that I am the vanquisher. In return for this service, I promise to give you back the writing by which you agree to let me have your title and to serve me."

The prince put on his armour, jumped on his horse, and, going out of the town, called thrice on the Invisible Prince.

"Here I am," said a voice close to him. "What do you wish? I will do whatever you tell me, for it was you who saved my daughter from Koshchei, and that is a service I shall never forget."

Prince Slugobyl showed him the army he wished destroyed. The Invisible Prince whistled, and said—

"Magical horse with the golden mane, come to

me, not on the ground but through the air, quick as an arrow, nimble as the lightning's flash."

That moment, in the midst of a whirlwind of smoke, there came a magnificent horse of an iron grey colour, and with a golden mane. It flew like the wind. Fire came from its nostrils. Its eyes sparkled like stars, and its ears smoked.

The Invisible Prince jumped upon it, and said to Prince Slugobyl—

"Take my sword and go and exterminate the left wing, while I destroy the right and the centre."

So the two set off, each to his place, and attacked the enemy with fury. To the right and to the left the soldiers fell like mown down grass. The slaughter was dreadful. The soldiers fled in all directions, but the two princes pursued them, and only ceased their labour when there remained on the field of battle only the dead and the dying. Then the two returned to the town. When they came near to the palace they shook hands. The Invisible Prince disappeared, and Prince Slugobyl went back to his stable.

It chanced that the king's daughter had been in such trouble that she had not been able to sleep. So she had gone out upon her balcony, and from there she had observed all that had occurred. She had heard the conversation between the false prince and his servant. She had seen Slugobyl call the Invisible Prince to assist him, and she had seen him give his clothes and armour to the impostor, while he told him all that he had done during the night. The princess divined all, but she resolved to be careful, and not to speak till the right time.

The next day the king ordered that the victory gained by his guest over the hostile army should be celebrated by great festivities. Calling · his daughter to him at the banquet, he was about to give her to the false prince, when she, leaving the table, made her way among the servants, and embracing Slugobyl, who stood amongst them, brought him forward.

"My father," said she, "and all you who are here present, here is he who gained the victory, and whom Heaven has sent me to be my husband. He whom you have been honouring is nothing more than a vile impostor, who has robbed his master alike of his name and of his rights. Last night I could not sleep, and, going out upon my balcony, I saw things such as eye had never before seen, and heard things such as ear had never before been acquainted with. I will tell you all, but first of all command that traitor to show you the paper by which he claims to be what he pretends."

The false prince then produced the paper signed by his master, and it was found to contain these words—

"Let the bearer of this paper, the traitorous and

wicked servant of Prince Slugobyl, receive the
punishment he well deserves for his treachery.

(Signed),   PRINCE SLUGOBYL."

"What!" cried the traitor, "do you say that that
is what the writing means?"

"Yes," cried they all.   "That is what is here."

Then he threw himself at the king's feet and
begged for mercy, but he only received what he
deserved.   He was tied to four wild horses and
torn to pieces.

Prince Slugobyl married the princess.   I, who
tell you of these things, was there myself, and I
there drank wine and hydromel, but, though my
beard was wetted, none of the drink went into my
mouth.

PRINCESS MARVEL.

Upon an island in the midst of the sea dwelt a princess, and with her lived twelve female attendants. The princess was of extraordinary beauty. Her face was calm and lovely as the moon, her lips were rosy red, and when she spoke her voice was full of music. Her eyes were remarkable. If they looked upon one with favour, her glance filled him with delight; but if they were cast upon one in anger, he was at once changed into a block of ice. All the princess's attendants were very beautiful, and devoted to their mistress. In time the fame of the princess's extraordinary loveliness was spread abroad. Folk came from all parts to see her, and the island became full of people.

Many princes sought the princess in marriage, but she rejected them all. Those who took her refusal in good part returned to their homes safe and sound, but woe to him who endeavoured to obtain the hand of Princess Marvel by force! Having landed with an army on the island, he saw his soldiers miserably perish, and he himself, pierced by a glance from the princess's eye, became a block of ice.

One day the great ogre Koshchei, looking around the world, took it into his head to see. all the different kings, queens, princes, and princesses it contained.

All of a sudden his glance fell upon the island where dwelt the princess. He looked, and saw the twelve beautiful attendants, and in their midst the lovely princess, asleep. As she slept the princess dreamt of a man who wore gold armour, was mounted on a fiery charger, and who was armed with an invisible club, and she felt that she loved the chevalier more than life itself.

Meanwhile Koshchei had fallen deep in love with the princess. Stamping three times upon the ground, he was at once transported to the island, but the princess, when he presented himself, rejected him with scorn, for she felt that she could be the wife of none but him whom she had seen in her dream. As Koshchei was determined to carry off the princess by force, if need be, she assembled her troops, and went out to meet him. Koshchei with his poisonous breath laid all the troops prostrate on the ground in a deep sleep. The princess, however, escaped, for, casting one of her angry glances on Koshchei, he was turned into a block of ice, and the princess returned to her palace. Koshchei did not long remain in that condition. When the princess came to her palace she found all the people within it asleep, and Koshchei, following her there, and not

daring to appear before her for fear of again feeling
the power of her eyes, built a wall of iron around
the palace, placed a dragon with twelve heads at
its gate, and waited, thinking that the princess
would at length tire of being a solitary prisoner,
and would agree to become his wife.

All upon the island were asleep, save the princess
and Koshchei. Weeks and months passed away
and Koshchei came to the gate of the palace time
after time to tell the princess that he loved her,
that resistance must be vain, and that, as his wife,
she should be queen of all the underground world.
Princess Marvel, however, listened to him in
silence.

Solitary and sad, she thought of him she had
seen in her dream. She thought of his shining
armour, his fiery horse, his invisible club, and the
glances he had cast upon her, assuring her he loved
her. She was always thinking of him. One day,
as she looked out, she saw a cloud passing along the
sky, and said to it—

"Stop on your way through the blue sky, cloud,
and tell me where is he whom I love, and whether
he ever thinks of me."

"I do not know," said the cloud. "Ask the
wind."

The princess, seeing a breath of wind playing
amongst the flowers, said to it—

"Wind, you travel far and wide and are so

happy in your freedom, have pity upon me, who am so miserable and helpless. Tell me where is he whom I love, and whether he ever thinks of me."

"Ask the stars," said the wind. "They know more than I do."

Princess Marvel lifted up her eyes to the bright, shining stars, and said—

"Stars, that shine so bright, can you see my eyes so full of tears without having pity on me? Tell me where is he whom I love, and whether he thinks of me."

"You had better ask the moon," said the stars. "She knows more that goes on upon the earth than we do." .

Then Princess Marvel said to the moon—

"Beautiful moon, look on me for a moment, and tell me where is he whom I love, and whether he thinks of me."

"Princess," answered the moon, "I know nothing about your friend. Wait a few hours, and then you will see the sun. Ask him. There is nothing hid from him, and he will tell you all."

The princess waited till morning, and when the sun rose she said to him—

"Sun, look on me, and tell me where is my love, and if he thinks of me."

"Princess Marvel," replied the sun, "dry up your tears and take courage. The prince is coming to you. He has obtained the magic ring from the depths below; he has collected together an innumerable army to come to your rescue, and to punish Koshchei. All will, however, be useless unless the prince takes another course, for Koshchei can overthrow all the prince's forces. I will go to the prince and give him some advice. Good-bye. I go to him who loves you. Be of good cheer, for he will come and rescue you, and you shall be happy."

Then the sun looked down upon the country where Prince Junak, clothed in golden armour and mounted on a fiery horse, got ready his army to go and attack Koshchei. Three times had the prince seen the Princess Marvel in his dreams, and he loved her deeply.

"Leave your army," said the sun to him, "for it will be of no service whatever against Koshchei. You can only deliver the princess from him by killing him, and to learn how you are to do that you must go to old Yaga. She can tell you how he can be killed. I will tell you how to get a horse which will carry you direct to her. Go towards the east until you come to a vast plain in the middle of which grow three oaks. Near to these you will find in the ground an iron door. Open it, and in a corner you will find the horse and the invisible club, which you must have to effect your wishes. You will afterwards learn how to proceed."

Prince Junak hardly knew what to do, but at length he resolved to take the sun's advice, so he

took off the magic ring from his finger and threw it
into the sea. His army at once disappeared, and
the prince set out to go to the east. For eight
days he went on, and then he came to a large plain,
in the middle of which he found the three oaks of
which the sun had spoken. He saw the iron door,
opened it, and saw before him some winding steps.
He went down these till he came to another iron
door, which he likewise opened. Then he heard
the neigh of a horse in the distance. Twelve other
doors opened of themselves, and the prince at last
came to the horse, which had been confined there
during a great many ages by a magician. When it
saw the prince, the horse broke the twelve iron
chains that held it, and ran to him.

"Prince Junak," it said, "I have waited for
ages for such a man as yourself. Now I am ready
to bear you and serve you faithfully. Leap on my
back and grasp the invisible club which is attached
to my saddle. You will not, however, have to
wield it, for you have only to tell it what you want
done and it obeys you of itself. Now let us go.
Where shall I take you? Name the place you wish
to be at, and we will be off at once."

The prince leaped on the horse's back, grasped
the invisible club, and set out. The horse took its
course through the air, and towards sunset the
prince came to the borders of an immense forest in
which was the residence of the old Yaga. Huge

oaks stood all around. Not a bird sang, not an insect hummed, all was profound silence. The prince went on till he came to a hut which stood upon fowl's feet, and which kept turning round and round.

"Hut," said the prince, "turn your front towards me and your back to the forest."

The hut turned to him and stood still, and the prince, going in, found the old Yaga there. When she saw him, she cried out—

"Why are you come here, Prince Junak, where no one has ever before been?"

"You are a foolish witch to ask questions of me," said the prince, "and not to welcome me." Then the Yaga rose and got ready everything that the prince needed. When he had eaten and drunk and rested himself, he told her why he had come.

"You have undertaken a difficult thing, Prince Junak," said the Yaga, "and you will want all your courage to succeed. I will show you how to overcome Koshchei. In the middle of the ocean is the island of eternal life. In the centre of the island grows an oak, and under it is an iron coffer. In the coffer is a hare, under the hare is a grey duck, and under the duck is an egg in which is contained the life of Koshchei. If the egg is broken, Koshchei dies."

The Prince at once set off to seek the egg. He rode on his wonderful horse until he came to the seashore. There he found a large fish struggling in a net.

"Prince Junak," said the fish, "let me loose, and I promise you your kindness shall not be forgotten."

The prince took the fish out of the net and set it free. Then he stood upon the shore, and thought how he should reach the island of eternal life, whose rocks he saw afar off. As he stood silent and sad, his horse said to him—

"Prince, what is it you are thinking of, and why do you look so sad?"

"How can I be otherwise," answered the prince, "when I find my journey here all in vain? How can I reach the far-off island?"

"Mount upon my back," said the horse, "and I will carry you to it. Only hold on well."

The prince did as the horse told him, and the brave steed, plunging into the sea, carried him over to the island. When he had arrived there, the prince looked around him, and in the middle of the island he saw an immense oak. Going to it, the prince seized it, and, pulling with all his force, the oak was torn up by the roots. The tree groaned as the prince tore it from the earth. In the place its roots had occupied was a large hole in which was an iron coffer. When the prince opened the coffer out sprang the hare, and away flew the duck carrying the egg with it. The duck made towards the sea, and the prince, fearing he should lose the

egg, shot at the bird. It fell, and with it also fell
the egg into the sea. Then the prince gave a cry
of despair, and, running down to the shore, he looked
around to see if he could see anything of the egg,
but it was not to be seen. All of a sudden a large
fish made its appearance. " Prince Junak," it said,
" I have not forgotten the service you did me, for
which I now make you some return."

As it said this the fish placed the egg upon the
shore, turned, and disappeared in the sea. Junak
was delighted. He went to his horse, leaped into
the saddle, and set off to the island where the
Princess Marvel dwelt, carrying the egg with him.
When he came there he saw the immense iron wall
Koshchei had raised around the palace, and the
dragon which lay at the gate. Six of the monster's
heads were asleep, while the other six watched.
Then the prince commanded his invisible club to
slay it. The dragon became furious under the
blows. It could not see the club, and so could not
tell to what quarter to turn itself. It rolled about,
it turned its twelve heads here and there, it darted
forth its sharp tongues, but all to no purpose. At
length, in despair, it turned its rage upon itself, and
with its sharp claws tore itself to pieces. Then the
prince went in, and, dismounting and taking the
invisible club in his hand, he sought the princess.

" Prince," said she, when she saw him approach,
" I have seen how you have overcome the dragon,

but a still more terrible conflict awaits you with my cruel jailer, Koshchei. Be careful, I beseech you, how you engage with him, for, should you fall, I will cast myself down the steep precipice near the palace."

"Do not fear, Princess Marvel," replied he, "for I hold the life of Koshchei in my hand."

Then said he to the invisible club—

"Go, and lay on to Koshchei."

The club went and commenced to deal such blows upon Koshchei that the king of the underground world commenced to grind his teeth, to roll his eyes, and toss himself hither and thither. None else than Koshchei could have borne the blows for an instant. He looked around him but could see nothing, and his pain was so great that he howled so that the whole island rang again. At length he came to the palace, and there he saw Prince Junak.

"Ah!" said he, "you have put me to all this pain, have you?"

He was about to send his poisoned breath against him, when the prince suddenly squeezed the egg he had in his hand. The shell broke, the yolk sprang out and fell to the ground, and at the same moment Koshchei fell dead. As he did so all his enchantments ceased. All the people in the palace awoke, and the iron wall disappeared.

All then was happiness. In a few days the prince and the princess were married, and they lived joyfully all their days.

THE GHOST.

ONCE upon a time a poor scholar going to town chanced to come across the body of a man which had been cast by some one under the walls of the town near to the gate. The scholar had very little money in his pocket, but for all that he willingly paid for the body to be buried in a Christian manner, so that it might be protected from insult. Having seen to this, he said a few prayers over the grave, and then continued his journey.

It chanced that one day, as he passed through an oak-wood, he felt tired, and laid himself down to sleep under one of the trees. When he awoke, how astonished was he to find that his pockets were all full of gold! He called down blessings on the head of whoever it was that had done him this good turn, and went on. At length he came to the bank of a wide river too deep for him to ford. Seeing the money he had with him, two boatmen offered to row him across. He entered the boat, and the men rowed till they came to the middle of the river, when they set upon him, robbed him of his gold, and then threw him into the water.

Russian.

M

Almost insensible he was carried away by the
stream, but as he was floating along he found a log
of wood beside him. He clung to it, and, keeping
himself afloat by means of it, managed to scramble
to shore. The log, however, was not really what it
seemed to be. It was the spirit of the dead man
whom the poor scholar had buried, and now, when
he was on shore, the spirit spoke to him, and
said—

"I am the spirit of him whose corpse you honoured
with burial. I am grateful for what you did, and in
return I will teach you three things : how to change
yourself into a crow, a hare, and a roebuck."

Having acquired these strange powers, the poor
man went on his way. In time he came to the
court of a mighty king, in whose service he entered
as an archer. Now this king was the father of a
beautiful princess who lived alone in a castle on a
solitary island. The walls of the castle were of
copper, and in it was a sword of such an extraordinary kind that one could, by waving it in the
air, cut down a whole army at one sweep. It was
natural that the sword should be coveted by very
many, but no one durst venture upon the island to
endeavour to obtain it.

Now at the time that the poor scholar came to
the court, the king was sore troubled by his enemies,
who were invading his dominions. He had great
need of the sword, but how could he get it? He

determined to see whether there was any among his
subjects who would dare to go to the island, and so
he caused a proclamation to be published to the
effect that if any one would bring him the magical
sword he should receive his daughter in marriage
and succeed him on the throne.

For a while no one came forward, but at last the
scholar determined to make the attempt. Every one
was astonished at his audacity, but he boldly went
to the king and begged him to give him a letter that
he might deliver to the princess asking her to give
the sword to him. The king wrote the letter and
gave it to the man, who at once set out, making his
way through the forest. Unknown to him he was
followed at a little distance by another of the king's
archers who had determined to go after him and see
how he sped. To travel the quicker, the archer
assumed the shapes of a hare and a roebuck, as was
suited to the ground over which he had to pass, and
at last he came to the sea-shore. He then took the
shape of a crow, and, flying over the waves as
quickly as his wings would bear him, he at length
came to the island on which was the castle.

He landed, and, making his way to the castle,
entered and delivered the king's letter to the princess, begging her at the same time to let him have
the victorious sword. The beautiful princess, who
had lived so long without looking upon a stranger,
scanned the archer closely, and fell in love with him.

She inquired of him how it was that he had had the
courage to undertake a task from which others drew
back, and to come to the castle which had not been
visited by man for so many years, and the archer
told her all about himself and the wonderful powers
he possessed. The princess, asking him to give her
proof that what he said was true, and desiring him
to change himself into the various forms, the
archer immediately did as she desired, and a handsome roebuck gambolled and played around her.
As the princess stroked it she plucked a tuft of hair
out of the animal's coat, but the archer did not
notice it. Next he changed himself into a crow, and
flew about the room. The princess laid her hand
upon the bird, and, while she stroked it, contrived to
pluck some feathers out of its wing without the
archer noticing it. He last of all changed himself
into a hare, and again the princess plucked a tuft of
hair out of his coat unobserved.

Then the princess wrote a letter to her father,
delivered the sword to the archer, and dismissed him.

Taking the form of a crow, the man flew over
the sea, and, having reached the shore, he changed
himself to a roebuck, and ran till he came to the
forest. Then he changed himself into a hare, and
began to make his way as fast as possible through
the forest depths. Now, the archer who had followed him had seen all that he had done till he
came to the sea-shore to fly over to the castle. There

the man had stopped awaiting the other's return.
He saw him come back in the shape of a crow,
change himself into a roebuck, and again into a
hare. As the hare was making its way through the
forest the archer bent his bow, and discharged an
arrow so well aimed that the hare at once fell dead
to the ground. The archer came up to it, took the
letter and the sword, and set out to the palace.
When he arrived there he gave the king the sword,
and demanded the promised reward.

The king was delighted to find himself in possession of the sword which would destroy all his
enemies. He confirmed his promise of the reward,
leaped into the saddle, and set off to the place where
the hostile army was encamped. Scarcely had he
come near enough to distinguish the flags of the
enemy in the distance than he brandished the sword.
At every stroke fresh foes fell to the ground, and at
last the few of them that were left fled from the field
stricken with terror at their comrades' mysterious
fate. The king collected together the booty he
found in the enemy's camp, and, returning home,
sent to his daughter to tell her to come to his court
so that he might give her to the archer.

Meanwhile the poor fellow who had been slain
while he was travelling as a hare lay dead in the
forest under an oak-tree. All of a sudden, however,
he came to life again, and, looking around him, he
saw the spirit of the dead man, whose body he had

buried, standing near him. The spirit told him that it had witnessed what had befallen him, and had by the power it possessed called him back to life.

"The wedding of the princess," it said to the man, "is to be celebrated to-morrow, and if you would keep her you must go as fast as you can to the palace. She will know you as soon as she sees you, and you will also be recognised by the archer who so wickedly slew you."

So the young man lost no time, but went on to the palace. When he came to the court he found all the guests already assembled. He entered the room, and no sooner had the princess cast a glance on him than she knew it was he, and was beside herself with joy. As for the treacherous archer, he turned pale when he saw the man, whom he thought he had murdered, alive and well.

Then the man told all the company everything that had happened, and how the archer had slain and robbed him. The tale was so wonderful that the guests could scarcely credit it, so the man changed himself into a roebuck to show them that what he had said was true. Then the princess put her hand in her pocket and took out of it a tuft of hair which was found to exactly fit a bare place on the roebuck's coat. The man changed himself into a hare, and the princess again produced a piece of a hare's coat which exactly fitted a bare spot in the animal's skin. Lastly he changed himself into a crow, and the princess producing the feathers she had formerly plucked out of the bird, it was found that they were missing in its plumage.

When the king saw all this he required no further proof of the man's story, and he ordered that the treacherous archer should be at once led forth and put to death by being torn to pieces by four wild horses.

Within the palace all was joy and festivity. The archer married the princess, and they wanted nothing, for the wish of their hearts was obtained.

Printed by T. and A. CONSTABLE, Printers to Her Majesty,
at the Edinburgh University Press.